How to Get the Most out of Bible Study

How to Get the Most out of Bible Study

by Leo R. Van Dolson, Ph.D.

Pacific Press Publishing Association

Mountain View, California
Oshawa, Ontario

Portions of this book have been adapted from a previous work by the author, *Hidden No Longer,* © 1968 by Pacific Press

Library of Congress Cataloging in Publication Data

Van Dolson, Leo R.
    How to get the most out of Bible study.

    1. Bible—Study. I. Title.
BS600.2.V36   220'.07   79-90590
ISBN # 0-8163-0360-6

Table of Contents

1
Listen—
God's on the Line

For whom was the Bible written? It was written for you—that's right—*you*! It is not just for the pious intellectual or the Bible scholar who can read God's Word in the original languages, although it is, of course, for each of them as well as for you. But God meant for the Bible to be read and understood by everyone.

One of our problems in this scientific age is that we have been conditioned to think that only the trained expert "really understands." Or maybe that isn't the real problem—maybe it's only an excuse. Maybe we've just become used to letting the experts and the scientists do our thinking for us. Maybe we're just too used to being spoon-fed everything. It's easier that way! Consequently many of us shy away from anything that demands extra effort. We'd rather push a button.

And that's what seems to be happening with a large number of people who try to study the Bible too. Since it takes effort, they give up without finding the blessing that God has placed there for those willing to discover personally the value and experience the joy of in-depth Bible study.

Let's look in on four individuals who regard themselves as Christians and find out how each relates to the challenge and opportunity of personal Bible study.

Charlie. After a long, hard day Charlie sat down for a few minutes to study his Bible. It was quite late at night, and Charlie was worn out from his activities—particularly his school homework. He found it almost impossible to focus his mind on the words he was reading, even though he was a "straight-A" student. If the truth were known, his intellectual accomplishments sometimes got in his way as he attempted to study the Bible. You see, Charlie enjoyed philosophy and the study of contemporary theology. The subtle doubts that such study raised made it difficult for him to accept the Bible at face value. Besides, he had already determined pretty much what his goals and values would be in life, and consequently he found it difficult to accept anything that in any way contradicted these predispositions.

Shelley. Not far away, but much earlier that same day, Shelley picked up her Bible and began to read too. Shelley liked reading her Bible. She was convinced that it was the thing to do. Yet, to be truthful, Shelley was both shallow and superficial in her approach to religion. She loved the promises of the Bible but shied away from those passages which indicate that Christian faith grows through trials. The last thing Shelley wanted was trouble—trouble of any kind. To her, religion

8

was great as long as it fitted into her selfish purposes. Since what she was reading didn't fill this bill, she snapped her Bible shut and turned on the television.

Dizzy. This young man got a lot out of reading the Bible when he took the time. But Dizzy was easily distracted. After reading for a few minutes, he'd begin to think about the run-in he had with his boss last Friday or that he really should go out and mow the lawn. The porch needed painting, and he was worried about Ellen's headaches. As these thoughts began to crowd out the import of what he was studying, Dizzy carefully marked his place, laid the Bible on the end table, and went out to wash the family car.

Reddy. Dizzy's next-door neighbor, Reddy, got up that morning while the rest of the family was still alseep. Experience had taught him that he needed these early, quiet hours for Bible study before going to school. Whenever he neglected to do this, things just didn't seem to go right.

After a period of prayer in which he asked the Lord to help him understand what he was about to read, he opened his Bible to the place where he had left off the day before. Soon he was totally immersed in the thrill of personal discovery. Joy and peace filled his heart as he gulped down great drafts from the fountain of the water of life.

After a quiet period of meditation and study Reddy felt a surge of courage run through him. What a great day this would be! He was happy to be alive and particularly pleased that as a son of

God he could represent his Lord before his schoolmates and friends. He closed his Bible with the prayer that God would help him share what he had just learned with someone who particularly needed that which God had given him for this day.

Parable of the Sower. Any resemblance in the responses described above to Christ's parable of the sower is purely intentional. As we thoughtfully analyze Jesus' fascinating story, we discover that those who are exposed to the Word of God fall into four categories:

1. The careless, prejudiced, and indifferent (wayside hearers).

2. Those who are shallow and superficial (stony-ground hearers).

3. The easily distracted (thorny-ground hearers).

4. Those who are most receptive (good-ground hearers).

Charlie's case shows that the careless and indifferent approach to Bible study is actually worse than not studying at all. The wayside hearers who have such an attitude seem to approach their occasional contact with the Scriptures with this motto: "Blessed are those who expect nothing, for they shall not be disappointed." Price, prejudice, and preconceptions all stand in the way of actually understanding truth.

Shallow and superficial Shelley is really too self-interested to gain much from her study. She represents those who trust in themselves and their own good works to "get by" spiritually. They have no real intention of ever letting themselves be molded into the image of Jesus. The Bible is not simply a tranquilizing agent. It does impart peace—but by showing us how to overcome those things that destroy our peace.

If Dizzy were a girl, we'd call her a Martha. The cares of the world interfere with the task of gaining Christian victory. Martha represents those independent people who enjoy doing everything themselves. They're uncomfortable when they learn that it's impossible for humans in and of themselves to accomplish what is essential in salvation—that their only hope is in depending on what Jesus has already done for them, and continues to do in their lives.

There's nothing wrong with bedtime snacks, providing it's the Bible that you're snacking on. But too many, like Dizzy in our parable, use the Bible *only* for a quick bedtime snack and neglect putting it to the use for which it was intended—as our daily bread.

But we're all so busy. How can we actually find time for serious Bible study? Stop and think about what you actually do in one day's time. Is it all really essential? What would happen if we cut out the nonessentials? Wouldn't there then be time to accomplish everything that we know demands priority attention? Someone has said, "Life stripped to its essentials is freedom." Maybe that's one reason Jesus counseled, "The truth will make you free." John 8:32. Set aside a specific amount of

11

time each day for Bible study, and you'll find that this promise does work.

Good-ground hearers, like Reddy, not only are honest with themselves and earnestly interested in discovering God's will for their lives, but they've trained themselves to get the most out of the time they regularly set aside for Bible study. What is their secret? How can we grow in our ability to get the "meat" (solid food) rather than just the "milk" out of God's Word? Meat, of course, must be chewed and is harder to digest; but it takes an understanding of strong doctrine for us to become strong Christians.

Where Do We Begin? Obviously we begin with exposure to the Word. The more we develop the study habit, the easier it becomes to study. The first essential step, after praying that the Holy Spirit will guide and direct, is reading. Naturally there's a big difference between casual and careful reading. One problem with much of our Bible study is that we are so familiar with the *words* that we skim over them without giving enough thought to the *Word*—or what the words are actually trying to tell us.

John White, a former missionary in Latin America, reports that Roman Catholics and communists who study the Bible for themselves find it easier to grasp what a Bible passage is actually saying than do evangelicals. He attributes this unexpected fact to the mental blocks with which most evangelicals approach Bible study. *They think they already know.*

One way to help get around this problem of preconceived opinions about a Bible passage is to read it in a different version or, if possible, in a different language.

When you do this, it's surprising how fresh and meaningful the old words become. You begin to see concepts that you had never thought of before in connection with that passage, and you gain new insights into its value as applied to your own everyday problems and needs.

Willard Harley, Jr., in his impressive little volume entitled *Get Growing, Christian* concludes that "a Christian should be able to outline every book of the Bible from memory. He should be able to identify major personalities in the Bible and describe their contributions. He should be able to trace the life of Jesus Christ and outline the content of His sermons. Many Christians feel that such knowledge is reserved for pastors and theologians, but the Bible was written for everyone, and its content should be thoroughly absorbed by every Christian." That's quite a challenge, isn't it?

Putting What We Learn to Practical Use. Of course it's not enough to understand fully what God wants us to know. Unless we, by His grace and power, put to work in our personal lives those precious truths He has revealed as a result of careful study and exciting discovery, we're probably better off if we never become involved in the search for God's will.

Second Timothy 3:16, 17 lists the reasons why

God's Word is valuable to us. Scripture is given for (1) doctrine, (2) reproof, (3) correction, and (4) instruction in righteousness. And the ultimate objective is "that the man of God may be complete, equipped for every good work." R.S.V.

You see, you're not just studying another textbook when you inductively approach the Bible. You're letting God tell you what He thinks is most important for you to learn about your life now and in the future.

He has much to tell you that's important and interesting.

Listen—won't you? God's on the line.

2
Ten Steps to Meaningful Bible Study

Jean Agassiz was not only a great scientist but a tremendously inspiring teacher. The following story, told by one of his students, has come to be regarded as a classic in introducing the basic principals of inductive study.*

A student of natural history enrolled under Agassiz, informing the professor that he was interested in all departments of zoology but especially in insects.

"When do you wish to begin?" Agassiz asked.

"Now," the student replied.

Removing a huge specimen jar from a shelf, the professor said, "Take this fish and look at it; we call it a haemulon (hem-yú-lon). By and by I will ask what you have seen."

He gave the student specific instructions on how to care for the specimen and left, leaving behind a very disappointed budding entomologist who couldn't understand why he had been assigned a fish to study.

*Based on the story entitled "The Student, the Fish, and Agassiz," *American Poems,* pp. 450-454.

In about ten minutes the student decided he had seen all there was to see in that fish and went in search of the instructor to inquire what to do next. But the professor had left the museum, and the student could do nothing but return to gaze steadfastly at his mute companion. After about an hour the fish began to look loathsome. He turned it over and around, looked it in its ghastly face. No matter how he looked at it, it seemed uninteresting to him. Deciding it was almost lunchtime—although only about eleven o'clock—he replaced the fish in its jar and enjoyed the respite of a lengthy lunch period.

When he returned, the student learned that Professor Agassiz had been at the museum but had left again and would not be back for several hours. Finally he mustered enough courage to study the fish again. He felt its teeth to see how sharp they were and then began to count the scales. Then a happy thought struck him—draw the fish. As he went about his drawing, he was surprised to discover new features in the creature.

It didn't seem long until the professor returned. Noting that the student was busily engaged in his drawing, he commented, "That is right. A pencil is one of the best eyes."

Then Agassiz asked, "Well, what is it like?"

The student eagerly rehearsed the structural details, only to be both astounded and disappointed at his instructor's evaluation.

"You have not looked very carefully," the professor commented earnestly. "Why, you haven't seen one of the most conspicuous features which is as plainly before your eyes as the fish itself. <u>Look again! Look again!</u>" And, with that parting advice, Agassiz left the student to his misery.

But the student had been inspired to new effort and soon began to realize how just his instructor's criticism had been. Toward the close of the afternoon the professor returned. "Do you see it yet?"

"No," was the reply, "I'm certain I don't. But I do realize how little I saw before!"

"That's next best. Put away your fish and go home. Perhaps you'll be ready with a better answer in the morning. I'll examine you then before you look at your fish."

The student was dumbfounded. Not only must he think of that fish all night, but the next day he must take an examination without a chance to review his discoveries. He passed a restless night, but early in the morning he seemed to sense the answer that he supposed the professor was looking for.

The next morning Professor Agassiz seemed eager for his student to see what he saw. To his anxious inquiry the student replied, "Do you perhaps mean that the fish has symmetrical sides with paired organs?"

"Of course! Of course!" The professor seemed thoroughly pleased, and proceeded to deliver a lecture on the importance of this point.

The student at last ventured a question concerning what he was to do next and was chagrined

17

at the answer, "Oh, look at your fish!"

For three long days the fish was placed before the student's eyes, and the young man was forbidden to look at anything else. Repeatedly Agassiz emphasized, "Look, look, look!" And the student later came to realize that this was the best lesson in "entomology" he ever received.

The fourth day a fish of the same group was placed beside the first, and now the student was required to note comparisons of resemblance and difference. Others followed, until a legion of jars covered the table and the odor from those jars had become a pleasant perfume to him.

Agassiz' training in the methods of observing facts and their orderly arrangement was always accompanied by his urgent exhortation not to be content with them; and the student concluded after eight months of such study, "It was almost with reluctance that I left these friends and turned to insects, but what I gained by this outside experience has been of greater value than years of later investigation in my favorite groups."

In this story can be found the basic outline to be followed in any scientific investigation. The scientific approach involves the three following steps: (1) observe, (2) interpret, and (3) apply.

When we apply these three steps to Bible study, we not only learn to discover truth for ourselves but find that nothing else can compare with the satisfaction that comes from personal discovery.

In the introduction to her book *The Joy of Discovery,* Oletta Wald reports her experience with this kind of Bible study. "I had been a student of the Bible several years before I learned how to study the Bible by myself. I could follow the suggestions of others and answer the questions which they asked, but I floundered when I tried to launch out for myself. I did not know where to start or what to do. I did not seem to have the insight that others had. The treasures of the Bible seemed locked behind abstract words. I always had to depend on someone else to open the door. While a student at the Biblical Seminary in New York, I was taught how to explore the truths of the Bible in a methodical and systematic way, I learned the precise steps to take when studying a passage. I found that it was like working a combination lock. When I followed the steps, the Word opened up to me. I felt free. I realized that I was no longer dependent on others in order to gain insights into Scripture. In a new way, Bible study became more meaningful and personal. Most of all it was deeply satisfying to know *how* to discover the deep truths in God's Word."

Long ago counsel came to Adventists to discover and understand for themselves the truths God has placed in His Word. The following quotation is only one of many which might be cited. "We should take one verse, and concentrate the mind on the task of ascertaining the thought which God has put in that verse for us. We should dwell upon the thought until it becomes our own, and we know 'what saith the Lord.' "—*The Desire of Ages,* p. 390.

19

As we go about doing this, there is a simple method that follows the scientific approach suggested earlier. To follow such methods does not mean that we are neglecting the guidance of the Holy Spirit. Without the Spirit's guidance we cannot ever expect to understand fully the significance of Bible truth, for it is through the gift of the Spirit of truth that we are guided into all truth. The danger, of course, is that with too much emphasis on the method, the purpose involved may be lost. However, if you will practice the method enough so that it becomes second nature, you will soon be caught up in the enthusiasm for Bible study that comes from a confidence that you can, with the Holy Spirit's aid, understand the Bible and discover truth for yourself.

The steps which follow are not essentially new. Most who read this will realize that they have been more or less using some, or perhaps even all, of these techniques for years. The value of this plan derives from an organized step-by-step method that anyone can use and which has been proved successful by persons of many denominations and backgrounds. Although the arrangement is my own, I claim no credit as originator. A quick glance at the bibliography will demonstrate the availability of many fine sources in the field of Bible study to which I am, of course, greatly indebted for my own approach. After having used these techniques for a number of years, I find it is not always possible to identify sources from which these ideas have come, but an effort will be made to give credit where credit is due.

The following specific steps are recommended in this approach, though there is always room for some variation.

no secrets

1. **Prayer.** Because the finite mind, without the guidance of the Holy Spirit, cannot possibly grasp the deep and meaningful truths of revelation which concern the character or works of the Infinite One (see Job 11:7, 8), it is essential that the first step in any approach to Bible study be prayer for guidance, which God has promised to those who ask in faith. Ellen G. White emphatically states: "Never should the Bible be studied without prayer. Before opening its pages we should ask for the enlightenment of the Holy Spirit, and it will be given."—*Steps to Christ,* p. 91.

2. **Reading.** The next step, one often hastily attended to, is that of actually reading the Bible. This step includes reading not only the specific passage involved but also the context, along with other Bible passages possibly essential to the understanding of the portion being emphasized in the study.

First of all, it is best to read the whole Bible book involved in the study at one sitting to get the overall picture and sense the total message and its impact. Then the specific portion being studied should be read several times, and anything which stands out in the text or particularly catches the attention of the reader should be marked or noted.

3. **Background Study.** In a later section a specific guide for background study will be given. Using some such guide, the Bible student should first seek to answer the questions of authorship and purpose from his own understanding based on the Bible reading he has just completed.

Of course, no one can fully understand the archaeological, chronological, and historical backgrounds of a Bible book in this way. Therefore, after you have found as many answers for yourself as possible to the questions suggested in the background study guide, you should then turn to source materials to fill out the missing or sketchy items of information. For instance, take Habakkuk. The book itself is practically our only source of information about the author; but most of the historical or chronological information concerning the time in which he lived and the events which shaped his ministry would, of necessity, have to be supplied from a good Bible commentary or Bible dictionary.

4. **Overall View.** Since the passage being studied is probably a portion of a larger book or grouping of books, it can best be understood in its relationship to the whole. The next step indicated, then, must be to obtain a general understanding of the author's viewpoint and purpose and of the way the book is structured to meet this purpose. A simple basic outline or one of the summary charts to be introduced later may be helpful in taking this step.

5. **Observations and Questions.** It is at this

point that real analysis begins. The four previous steps suggested are preliminary, yet essential, in preparing the way to make the study most rewarding and meaningful and in leading eventually to the personal discovery of what the Bible is really saying. You need to train yourself through practice to become a careful observer, for this next step is the critical one which determines success or failure.

Several charts which can be used effectively will be described in some detail in later chapters. The choice of which to use generally depends on the size of the Scripture portion being studied and the specific objective of the study.

In general, observations made about the passage under this step should be more than the trite, superficial type which most people usually settle for in personal Bible study. They should reflect careful and prayerful attention to every word, phrase, and implication of the text being studied. A new version of the Bible which is not familiar to the reader or a foreign-language translation can be particularly helpful in that these will help you to view the familiar passage in a fresh and interesting way and to approach your study from the viewpoint of one who has never heard these things before.

You should record these observations immediately before they are forgotten. Questions of clarification of words, phrases, and passages will naturally arise as one studies in this observant way. These, too, should be written down before they are forgotten. Do not ask questions for questions' sake, as this may lead to irrelevant ideas and sidetrack the study. The questions, when answered, must really clarify the meaning of the text.

Particularly important are questions that deal with definitions, reasons, implications, relationships, and progression. At this point do not spend time looking up answers. If the answer is not readily apparent, go on with the observation-type study. Many of the questions will be cleared up as your study progresses.

6. **Review.** After the above methods have been carefully applied to the section being studied, it is time once again to take an overall look at the materials now compiled. Go back over the materials, reading observations made and doing your best to answer questions raised. In the light of your total understanding of the section being studied, you should now be surprised at how many of your questions you are really able to answer.

7. **Comparisons.** Next a little additional thought and study will help you to find the relationship of the passage under study with preceding or following passages or with other Scripture references containing similarities or differences. These comparisons should also be noted, and a simple chart will help you to organize these thoughts more clearly.

8. **Summary.** After analysis comes synthesis. Check once again the summary chart or outline

constructed under step 4. Add to this or alter it to suit your advanced understanding of the material you are studying. This step is important in giving depth, purpose, and significance to your study. Without this effort at summarization you are likely to get yourself bogged down in words, phrases, and verses which may be exceedingly interesting in themslves but not wholly significant unless understood in the light of the entire passage. Try summarizing the meaning of the section being studied in just a few words or sentences.

9. **Check Authorities.** Now, at long last, you are probably thinking, is the time to turn to authorities. You have done all you can and gone as far as you can on your own. But the job is not finished yet. You are now eager to test your own discoveries and ideas against those of scholars who have spent many years in study. And you will undoubtedly be surprised to note that you have come up with many ideas that they have found. Perhaps you will also find areas of disagreement. Don't be quick to discard your own findings. In many cases your opinion is as good as anyone else's—and is, of course, more personally meaningful since it is your own.

You will be thrilled to discover occasionally, as all do who persist in this type of study, that you have discovered something no one else has thought of. This is the greatest evidence of the value of this kind of study; and the more you attempt it, the more such discoveries will come.

Seventh-day Adventists will, of course, turn to what we consider an inspired commentary—the writings of Ellen G. White—and your faith in these writings will grow as you see how clearly she understood the deep significance of biblical passages. Commentaries, dictionaries, and source books will also be helpful in answering many of the questions you have not been able to answer for yourself.

One of the greatest benefits of group study comes at this point; for as you share your new insights with others who have been studying in the same way, your own understanding will be enlarged, and the verbal expression of your own thoughts will help you understand your ideas even more clearly. If your study has been thorough, it will be hard not to share your discoveries with others; and your own enthusiasm will in turn generate enthusiasm on their part. You will also find that they have probably been able to answer questions you could not. At least group discussion will clarify many of the issues involved. Add all these shared discoveries to your own notes to make them more complete.

10. **Application.** This final step is in reality the most important step, and personal Bible study is not really of value to us until we apply the truths being discovered to our own lives and circumstances. Oletta Wald states in this connection: "You can teach yourself to become a profoundly intellectual Bible student and yet miss the ultimate purpose of all Bible study: to permit the

Word of God to speak in a personal way to your heart. To observe the facts and to interpret the facts are only the first two steps in the process of Bible study. There is little value gained unless you follow the third step: to apply the truths to your own life."—*The Joy of Discovery,* p. 42.

Specific suggestions on how to take this final step of application will be given later in this book.

The foregoing ten steps are not ten hard-and-fast commandments to be slavishly followed in Bible study. Never let a method get in your way. What counts is that you're learning to get more out of your current approach to study than you ever have before. These ten suggestions have grown out of several years of using this approach and can be adapted to varying situations and circumstances in the study of particular passages.

For instance, if you already clearly understand the background and authorship of a Gospel like that of John and have read it many times in recent years, it would not be necessary to spend much time on steps 2 and 3, which involve reading and background study. To do so might just cause you to bog down in rather boring repetition of the thoroughly familiar. Of course, if you never have carefully analyzed the Gospel before but have depended on what others have said or written, you will find it tremendously stimulating to do a personal analysis and come this way to a better understanding of the author and his purpose.

Following the ten steps suggested until they become second nature will lead you to a more meaningful approach to uncovering the hidden treasures God has for you in His Word. We will go into more detail about the excitement of the search for hidden treasure in the chapter that follows.

3
Treasure
Hid in a Field

Under the sponsorship of wealthy Lord Carnarvon, Howard Carter engaged in archaeological exploration in the area of Thebes off and on beginning in 1908. The two had been responsible for several interesting discoveries, but World War I nearly stopped their explorations. From 1919-1921 Carter worked over the entire section of the Valley of the Kings between the tombs of Merneptah, Ramses III, and Ramses IV. Still no important discovery was made, and the concession to dig there had only a few more weeks to run.

Carter had just about given up hope of making any major discovery in that area when on the morning of November 4, 1922, he found a rough-hewn stairstep below the entry to Ramses IV's tomb. Following this lead, he uncovered the entrance to another royal tomb—one that was to prove more fabulous in the richness of its contents than any other Egyptian royal sepulcher uncovered in modern times. As he came to the last barrier across the passageway, Carter was able to read the hieroglyphic inscription, which indicated that the occupant of the tomb was the long-sought Tutankhamen.

Excitedly, Carter summoned Lord Carnarvon from England. The wealthy patron and his daughter arrived in Alexandria on November 20, and on November 25 the first stone was removed from the tomb wall, allowing Carter, Lord Carnarvon, and Carnarvon's daughter, Lady Evelyn Herbert, to catch the first breathtaking glimpse of the strange golden animals, statues, and furniture that have now become world famous. The treasure they discovered that memorable day is said to be one of the greatest single discoveries of concentrated wealth.

Late in the nineteenth century an Egyptian woman, rummaging in the ruins of Amarna, discovered a large number of ancient letters in the Akkadian language, written on baked clay tablets. Stuffing them in gunnysacks, she sold them for a pittance to a local tradesman. The tradesman loaded the gunnysacks on donkeys and gave them a rough 200-mile ride to Cairo. It was an unprofitable trip for him, however, as the Cairo antiquity dealers refused to buy them, being suspicious that they were forgeries, since no clay tablets written in cuneiform had ever been found in Egypt.

The sacks of tablets were next reloaded on the same tradesman's donkeys and transported to Luxor, 400 miles south of Cairo. By the time a scholar in Luxor recognized their value, many of the tablets had been broken. They were soon purchased, however, by museums; and an astonished world learned that hundreds of these were actually letters—diplomatic correspondence and dispatches from officials in western Asia to kings of the Egyptian Amarna period. The Amarna letters, as they are now known, are dated about 1400-1360 B.C., which is the approximate time of the Israelite invasion of Canaan under Joshua. They shed valuable light on conditions in Palestine and Egypt at that time. These little gray tablets greatly enlarge the Bible student's understanding of events only hinted at in the Old Testament.

In Palestine the greatest archaeological discovery to date has been that of the Dead Sea Scrolls. At the foot of a rugged cliff, on a whitish-brown terrace looking down toward the Dead Sea, is a place known today as Khirbet Qumran (Ruins of Qumran). Sometime during the latter half of the second century B.C. a community of Essenes separated themselves from the orthodox Judaism of Jerusalem and moved to the site. By the spring of 31 B.C. a sizable community had grown up there. It was destroyed by an earthquake, the effects of which can still be seen in the ruins. After that calamity the site remained uninhabited for a time; but finally the Essenes came back and repaired the buildings, adding some new construction.

About A.D. 68 this community was destroyed again, this time by the Romans during their campaign in Judea to quell the first Jewish revolt. The members of the community fled, hiding their precious library in nearby caves. Valuable scrolls were wrapped in linen and placed in earthenware jars in what is known today as Cave 1. The mouth of the cave was then sealed with rocks. This library was probably first uncovered in the eighth century, when most of the books were taken to Jerusalem and subsequently lost.

One day in 1947 a young Bedouin, Muhammed Adah-Dhib, was searching for his lost goat in the hills and cliffs behind Khirbet Qumran. In one cliff he noticed a strangely placed hole which seemed to lead into a cave. Picking up a stone, he threw it into the cave. The boy was surprised to hear the sound—one quite familiar to him—of pottery being broken. Muhammed's curiosity being aroused, he pulled himself up to the small cave entrance and peered in. Inside he saw several large, wide-necked jars. Being afraid to enter the cave alone, he returned to the Bedouin camp; and the next day he returned to the cave with an older friend. The two squeezed their way through an opening into the cave and found several two-foot-high earthenware jars. They tried to sell the scrolls they found in those jars to an antiquities dealer in Bethlehem for $56. He was not interested, not realizing that in a few years just five of those eleven scrolls would bring the fabulous price of $250,000. Two of the discovered scrolls have proved to be Hebrew manuscripts of the book of Isaiah, older by a thousand years than any Old Testament Hebrew manuscripts previously known. It is generally agreed that at least one of these scrolls was written about the second century B.C.

One of these scrolls is the complete text of the book of Isaiah and is known technically as IQIs[a]. This manuscript seems to be somewhat older than the second, known as IQIs[b]. This second manuscript is written in beautiful handwriting by a more experienced scribe, but unfortunately it is only fragmentary.

These scrolls demonstrate that our present Bible text of Isaiah has come down to us practically unchanged since the time of Christ and before. They also present impressive evidence that the book of Isaiah was the work of just one author instead of two, as is so often claimed, for there is no evidence in either scroll that Isaiah ever existed as two separate books or as the work of two different authors. It seems to have been regarded as a single unit, the work of one author, centuries before Christ.

The great thrill to the student of prophecy regarding the discovery of the Isaiah scrolls comes from the fact that Bible prophecy has been verified and reaffirmed. That is because the Messianic prophecies of Isaiah have been shown to have been written in the very form in which we now have them before the time of Christ. The accurate and detailed fulfillment of these Messianic prophecies in the life of Christ not only provides evidence that He is the Son of God and Saviour of the world, but demonstrates the truth and reliability of other prophecies given by God in the Bible.

These thrilling discoveries, and many more that cannot here be recounted, have opened new vistas of understanding of the past. What is more important to the Bible scholar, these discoveries in Bible lands have illumined and enlarged our understanding of the Holy Scriptures and have combined with other areas of research to demonstrate fallacies and mistaken viewpoints of Bible critics.

Not many will ever have the opportunity of becoming biblical archaeologists, but all can share the thrill and joy of biblical discovery. Often we hear it repeated that the Bible is an inexhaustible treasure chest overflowing with glorious gems of truth. However most people who study the Bible seem content merely to glance briefly across the picked-over surface of this treasure without ever becoming fully aware of the excitement and pleasure that comes from personal discovery of hidden gems beneath.

In His parable recorded in Matthew 13:44, Christ likens the "kingdom of heaven" to a treasure hid in a field. This parable is based on a rather common occurrence in the Palestine of Christ's day. It was a time when no such structures as modern bank vaults existed. Thefts, robberies, and invasions with their resultant pillaging and plundering were frequent. Therefore, those who had valuables worth trying to preserve often followed the custom of burying them in the earth— either in the earthen floors of their houses or somewhere in their fields. If, however, the individual or individuals who hid the family treasure were slain in the invasion by marauding armies or captured and exiled, the place where the treasure had been concealed might be soon forgotten. So it was not uncommon in the time of Christ for someone to uncover such buried treasure.

In the mind's eye we can picture the scenes described in this brief parable. A man is working his neighbor's field on shares. He doesn't have and can't afford land of his own. One day he is plowing the field when, suddenly, the plow strikes something hard and metallic. He stops the oxen and quickly gets down on his hands and knees and scoops up the dirt. In a few moments he has uncovered a small treasure chest and, as he breaks it open, recognizes that it contains a fortune in coins and jewels far exceeding anything he has ever hoped to own. But according to the laws of that country, it isn't his unless he owns the field. Quickly he covers it up, marking the spot, and runs over to his neighbor's house.

"Neighbor," he says, trying to hide his excitement, "I would like to buy your field. How much will you take for it?"

"I'm sorry, friend. It is not for sale. This property has been in my family for generations, and I don't want to sell it."

But the man will not take No for an answer. He insists and insists until finally the neighbor, in order to get rid of him, places a ridiculously high price on the field.

"All right, I'll buy it! Give me until three o'clock

this afternoon to raise the money."

Quickly he runs home and begins taking stock of all his resources. Naturally he doesn't have enough. Immediately this man, who must buy the field to own its treasure, begins selling his furniture. He's in such a rush that he has no time to explain to his wife what he's doing. Soon the furniture is gone, and still he's far short. He remembers a friend who has been wanting to buy his house; and because he is willing to settle for a fraction of its worth, the friend is able to pay him cash. Still there isn't enough! He goes back and strips the house, even selling every bit of clothing but that which he and his family are wearing. His wife's precious dowry goes—everything. She is terribly upset, but he has no time to argue with her. Still there is more to raise. Without a moment's hesitation he borrows the remaining amount at a usurious rate of interest promising to sell himself and his family into slavery if he cannot make the payments.

Finally he has enough, and it's almost three o'clock. Without a word of explanation to anyone he races back to his neighbor's house and completes the transaction for the field. By now his wife has gathered her parents and her in-laws and several of her close friends; and they are weeping and wailing, for they are sure he has gone stark, raving mad. They follow him at a safe distance as he races back to the field. Now they're certain of his insanity as they see him get down on his hands and knees and begin to paw up the earth. But in just a few moments their mourning turns to shouts of rejoicing as he presents them with his newfound treasure, now his to keep.

The story is not told to teach us how to take advantage of our neighbors. The point that Jesus is making is that when we find hidden treasure worth far more than anything we ever expected to find or have, we joyfully give all that we have for it.

Tremendous joy comes in discovering the hidden treasures of the Word of God. The reward we receive is worth far more than the effort it takes to discover it. And the effort itself becomes joyful, just as with the man in the parable who became so thrilled that in his joy he went and sold all that he had. The effort and trouble that it took to sell his things quickly, even at a loss, was no bother to him but was exciting in itself as he anticipated the final results.

Since the joy and thrill of discovery are so rewarding, why is the search for the diamonds of truth to be found in the Bible treasure chest so neglected? Because *work* is involved. Anything worthwhile takes effort, of course. And how much we miss if we are unwilling to put forth the effort.

A truly stupendous privilege is involved—the privilege of sharing God's truth as He reveals it to you in a way as meaningful as if the words recorded hundreds and even thousands of years ago had been placed in the Scriptures and preserved for just this one moment of time—the thrilling moment of your personal discovery.

Naturally you cannot fairly expect the deepest and most satisfying discoveries at first or all at once.

Even after the thrill of discovering the Messiah, it took the disciples quite a while to recognize how unique and precious this discovery really was. Likewise it takes a little training, a little experience, a little discipline to discover and recognize Bible truth for yourself; but the results are sure. God Himself guarantees this in His promise "And ye shall seek me, and find me, when ye shall search for me with all your heart." Jeremiah 29:13.

Now, how do we go about discovering the hidden treasure God is anxious to share with us? You'll recall that in chapter 2 we began with prayer and thoughtful Bible reading. The next step suggested was to get involved in thorough background study—to find out what the author was actually thinking about so that we can more adequately think his thoughts after him. One way of accomplishing this will be outlined in the chapter that follows.

4
Let the Author Say What He Wants

In 1973, on Yom Kippur, an especially sacred day when Jews can be found in the synagogue and secular activities in Israel cease, Arab forces began a sudden, unannounced attack.*

Army reservists, rushing for the front lines, put special emergency signs on their buses and trucks to keep the Orthodox Jews from stoning them for violating this most sacred day.

Most astounding was that the Israelis had been caught unprepared. The Arab forces caught them completely off guard, trapping Israeli soldiers inside their undermanned Bar Lev line forts on the Egyptian front and overwhelming Israeli outposts along the Syrian border. In the two previous Middle-East wars, of 1956 and 1967, the Israelis' cannily detailed foreknowledge of the Arab's intentions had led to the quick defeat of Arab forces. But now they had been caught napping. Why?

*Paraphrased here, with permission, from David B. Tinnin with Dag Christensen, *The Hit Team* (New York: Dell Publishing Co., 1976), pp. 206-209.

One reason was that Israeli intelligence was concentrating its efforts on trying to stop terrorism in Europe. Yet only two days before the war began, an Israeli secret agent delivered a complete copy of the Egyptian-Syrian war plan, including the outlines of a surprise attack to take place at dawn on Yom Kippur. It was so secret that only twenty to twenty-five leaders in Egypt and Syria knew about it.

Golda Meir, the prime minister, was not convinced, however, that the information was genuine; and army officers, jealous of the Mossad (secret service), supported her view. It wasn't until they were caught by surprise and the attack unfolded exactly according to that very war plan that Israeli leaders belatedly realized what a tragic blunder they had made.

A prevalent human tendency accepts only those facts which seem to fit preconceived opinions. This is one reason, at least, why there are so many interpretations and different understandings of the Scriptures.

We must learn to "let the author say what he wants to say." This is easy to say and easy to agree with, but very difficult to practice. You probably have seen the placard which reads, "I know you believe you understood what you think I said. But I am not sure you realize that what you heard is not what I meant!" This highlights the problems inherent in understanding what others write and say and are attempting to communicate.

Adventists are prone to condemn other religions as being "blind" to what the Bible really says. But isn't there a possibility that we, too, have our blind spots? Did Christ eat meat? (Somehow we except fish from the category!) Did He ever partake of the lamb that was served with the Passover meal? It would be difficult to believe that He didn't. Yet somehow those of us who have been given special instruction not to eat such food as a means of preserving health in these last days—physically, mentally, socially, and spiritually—seem to think that Christ, living in a different time and culture and under different circumstances, had to follow exactly the same dietary rules which God in His love has prescribed for our time. Even in early Christian times, with the apostles still alive, the church was troubled by differences of opinions on some matters of teaching and practice. Can we expect Adventists all over the world today, with vast differences in culture and background, all to follow exactly the same practices and understand every teaching in exactly the same way? Obviously there is room for differences in interpretation and practice in spite of general agreement on basic principles and fundamental doctrines.

It really does not matter whether or not the Bible author (and by the use of this term I refer to the prophet who actually wrote the words that were recorded for us) agrees with what you would like him to say or with your preconceptions of what you think he should say in the specific circumstances in which he is writing. If you are to be able to understand fully what he intends, you must grant him the right to say what he wants to say in his own way of expression. Also you must make a special attempt to understand exactly what he is saying rather than to make an attempt to read into it your own concept of what he should have written.

A type of chart which is particularly designed to help us bring into sharp focus what an author intends to put across is that which is known as the horizontal summary chart.

The horizontal summary chart is not just an outline. It combines all the features of an outline along with a structural portrait of the Scripture division being studied. It also attempts a brief paraphrase in one's own language, which is valuable in really understanding what the Bible is saying. Oletta Wald, discussing summarization by means of charts, points to the importance of this technique as follows:

"The chart is one of the most effective ways to enable you to grasp the whole picture of a chapter or book. It has real value as a study device and equal value as a teaching tool. . . . A chart is a graphic and visual way of blocking out the material which you are studying so that content and relationship can more easily be seen and understood. The purpose of your chart will determine the kind you use and the material which you record."—*The Joy of Discovery,* p. 38.

The basic form for the horizontal summary chart follows:

TEXT—Subtitles		

BOOK (or textual reference)—TITLE

Verse or Paragraph TITLE—Brief summary in own words of this section.		

If you are dealing with a chapter, the chart can be divided by paragraphs or by what seem to stand out as major divisions. Application of this chart to a chapter such as 1 Corinthians 13 is illustrated on page 44.

Note the following:

1. How simply and graphically, yet comprehensively, a whole chapter or section can be diagramed.

2. The use of lists and comparisons within the chart.

3. The recurrent use of the same word *love* in the subtitles to tie the chapter together.

4. The placement of verse indicators.

5. How the chart effectively presents both content and structure.

6. The technique of summarizing a section like verses 9 to 12 in just a few words of your own choosing.

1 Corinthians 13—THE GIFT OF LOVE

1-3 = OTHER GIFTS COMPARED WITH LOVE	POSITIVE STATEMENTS	NEGATIVE STATEMENTS	8b—TEMPORARY NATURE OF FIRST THREE GIFTS:
1. Tongues—without love = NOISE	1. Patient	1. Not Jealous	1. Tongues
2. Prophecy	2. Kind	2. Not Boastful	2. Prophecy
3. Understanding of mysteries and knowledge	3. Rejoices in Right	3. Not Arrogant	3. Understanding and Knowledge
4. Faith Without Love = NOTHING	4. Bears All Things	4. Not Rude	9-12 = REASON WHY THEY ARE TEMPORARY
5. Sacrifice	5. Believes All Things	5. Not Insistent on Own Way	Needed now due to lack of clear understanding we'll later have in God's presence
6. Martyrdom Without Love = Gain NOTHING	6. Hopes All Things	6. Not Irritable	13—THREE ABIDING GIFTS
	7. Endures All Things	7. Not Resentful	1. Faith
		8. Not Rejoicing at Wrong	2. Hope
		9. Never Fails	3. Love = GREATEST

This kind of chart can be used in exactly the same way to outline a larger section or even a Bible book. In the case of some of the longer Bible books, however, your basic divisions should be groups of chapters rather than verse or paragraph divisions. A summary chart of this kind should never include more than five or six subdivisions at most, or you'll negate one of its greatest values—that of being able to picture a whole chapter, section, or book of the Bible in a one-page chart which enables you to take in the whole thing at one glance.

When studying a Bible book or passage, it is obviously essential to find out everything possible about the author and the times in which he was writing as well as the particular circumstances that called for the message that he was directed to present. How can we really understand Jonah's attitude toward Nineveh and the Assyrians unless we understand the aggressiveness and cruelty they exhibited toward Jonah's people? Or how can we understand what it meant for Abraham to leave Ur and wander as a nomad without a home unless we have at least a brief acquaintance with the amazing civilization and culture of the highly advanced Mesopotamian city in which he spent the first seventy-five years of his life? The more we understand about the background and times of a particular Bible passage, the better we can grasp the intent and depth of the writer's message.

The following guide has been prepared to help

you ferret out those aspects of authorship and purpose which are most important in understanding Bible backgrounds. Naturally, not every question can be answered for each book or passage that you might study. There are just some things that we no longer know about Bible times or personalities. But you should attempt to answer just as many of the questions listed as you possibly can.

It is best, first, to try to answer as many as you can from your own personal knowledge or from careful observation of the section of Scripture that you are studying. When you have done as much as you can, then you must turn to authorities and historical and archaeological studies that will give you the best information available. The spirit of prophecy writings provide, of course, an incomparable source, but they should not be used to the exclusion of all other study. Bible dictionaries and Bible commentaries can be most helpful in your search. Be sure to get the latest information available, as new discoveries about Bible backgrounds are continually being made. The Seventh-day Adventist Bible student will want to use caution when consulting those works that reflect liberal or critical viewpoints which we believe distort the accuracy of these sources.

Choose a Bible book to start with for which there is much available information concerning the author and background. You might try doing your background study on the book of Romans, for instance. Then, from personal observation of what is contained in the book and from other sources such as *The Acts of the Apostles* by Ellen G. White and the *S.D.A. Bible Commentary,* seek answers to the following questions:

Background Study Guide

1. Authorship:
   a. Who was the author?
   b. At what time in his life was he writing?
   c. Where was he when he wrote this material?
   d. What characteristics of the author are revealed here?
   e. What was he experiencing at the time?
   f. What is the underlying tone of the passage?
2. Purpose:
   a. What do historical records indicate as background for this section?
   b. What contribution do archaeological findings make?
   c. What is the author's primary purpose in writing this passage?
   d. What major truths or concerns and convictions does he present in order to bring out his purpose?
   e. How has he arranged his material to emphasize his purpose?
   f. What are the key words he uses?
   g. Who are the intended readers, and how does this affect his purpose?
   h. How does this emphasis compare with other works of this period (by the same author or other authors)?

5
Showers of Blessing

Think about the Bible for a minute. It's the all-time best seller. Why? One reason, of course, is that it contains God's messages to man and the truths He reveals about the kind of world and universe we live in. The Bible isn't made up of essays that contain what men think about God. Instead it contains the thoughts of God Himself as expressed through our fellow-servants the prophets.

But even that does not explain why the Bible enjoys a continuous popularity—a fact that has been noted ever since books were first printed. Another reason for the Bible's popularity is that it speaks clearly to the needs and heartfelt interests of men everywhere and always has since it was first initiated 2500 years ago.

These facts still leave some questions. Why is it that no matter how many times we read it or hear it read, the Bible still touches our lives so much? Why are we so interested in events and people whose setting and culture are so foreign and so far removed from us? Why do we spend time poring over the pages of a book that is written in what appears to us to be stilted, difficult, old-fashioned language?

To illustrate this last point, in the back of one of my King James Versions of the Bible is a glossary that lists 454 words that have changed meaning or fallen out of general use since that Bible was first published in 1611. Some samples follow. Why not indicate after each word what you think it means; then check the answers at the end of the chapter.

1. Affect.
2. Check.
3. Fat.
4. Fray.
5. Let.
6. Ouches.
7. Prevent.
8. Sith.

In spite of all the difficulty we sometimes have in understanding the King James Version and its culture and setting, many of the incidents recorded are among the best-loved stories of mankind; and the Bible is still one of the most-used books there is. Why?

Isn't it because it's full of human-interest stories, actual case histories, and real-life situations—with real-life people facing the same kinds of problems, frustrations, and decisions that we face today and finding their answers and the way through their problems in God's revealed will?

Stop and think—where would you go to find the comforting story of a seemingly innocent man

49

who unjustly suffered all kinds of trouble but never gave up his basic faith in the Lord? Of course he was discouraged and grumbled and complained at times, but he still ultimately clung to his faith in God.

Where would you go to find an account of a young man separated from his family ties and all that meant everything to him, unjustly accused and imprisoned, yet standing so squarely for his God and his beliefs that he was at last called to minister to the needs of a whole nation and did so most effectively?

Where can you find more thrilling true stories than these? Where else can you find such inspirational material to help you develop a strong confidence in God? Where else could a prisoner of war by the name of Howard Rutledge find the necessary inner resources to withstand the physical and psychological pressures exerted on him during the course of seven years of imprisonment in North Vietnam—five of which were spent in solitary confinement?

Howard attended a Baptist Sunday School as a boy growing up in Tulsa, Oklahoma, but as an adult had come to neglect completely the spiritual dimension of life until he found himself in solitary confinement in what was known by the American prisoners as Heartbreak Hotel.

As he began to realize the need for resources outside himself in order to stand what he was going through, Howard began to recall Scripture passages, choruses, hymns, and snatches of sermons he had been exposed to in those more carefree years in Sunday School. In his book *In the Presence of Mine Enemies** Howard reports that it wasn't too difficult to recall about three dozen songs, but then the going became harder. One night as the rains poured down and the lightning knocked out the lights, he remembered his thirty-seventh gospel song, "There Shall Be Showers of Blessing." This led him to remember another, a contrasting piece, "Heavenly Sunshine."

In the brief snatches of conversation the prisoners could get away with during the guards' less watchful moments, they would most often share recollections of Bible stories and Scripture passages. One day Harry Jenkins, who occupied a nearby cell, remembered the story of Ruth and Naomi. Even though the story was nearly three thousand years old, Howard confides that they lived off it for days, rethinking what it meant and how it could be applied to their current need.

These recollections enabled them to overcome the physical and psychological pressures to which they were subjected and to resist having their spirits crushed. Howard states that, as a youth, he had not seen the value or importance of memorizing Bible verses or hymns; but, when it was too late to do anything about it, he wished time and again that he had taken better advantage of his

*Howard and Phyllis Rutledge with Mel and Lyla White, *In the Presence of Mine Enemies* (Old Tappan, N.J.: Fleming H. Revell Company, 1973).

opportunity to memorize more verses that would have helped make his days bearable.

Much could be written about the neglect of the art of memorizing passages of Scripture. We know that the time will come when we will be forbidden access to God's Word, just as Howard was, and will be dependent on that which we have stored in our memories. But even just the act of mechanically memorizing texts can sometimes get in the way of our discovering for ourselves what God is trying to put across in a particular passage.

Note the following challenge: "There is but little benefit derived from a hasty reading of the Scriptures. One may read the whole Bible through and yet fail to see its beauty or comprehend its deep and hidden meaning. One passage studied until its significance is clear to the mind and its relation to the plan of salvation is evident, is of more value than the perusal of many chapters with no definite purpose in view and no positive instruction gained."—Ellen G. White, *Steps to Christ,* p. 90.

When we really learn to study the Bible so that we can take a single passage and find all that the Lord has put there for us to understand, there will be both a deepening of our spiritual experience and a hunger for continued study. It's always a blessing to listen to someone who is well versed in its study explain the Bible, but how much more exciting and stimulating it is to be able to discover the deep significance of a Bible passage for ourselves. Yet so many Christians today do not know how to do this and consequently do not appreciate the thrill and challenge of this kind of study.

A careless view of Bible study that often results is, of course, detrimental to Christian growth. Some of us, however, seem to approach the Scriptures with this attitude: "Blessed is he who expects nothing, for he shall not be disappointed." Yet the Holy Spirit longs to share precious treasures of truth with us if we will only devote some time and effort to our study. "Christ would have the searcher of his word sink the shaft deeper into the mines of truth. If the search is properly conducted, jewels of inestimable value will be found."—Ellen White, *Review and Herald,* July 12, 1898.

How do we go about the kind of study that will bring us such rich rewards in understanding the treasures of truth? As Ellen White suggests, the obvious point of beginning is to select a passage for study and concentrate on it until its significance is clear to the mind.

Concentrate first on the obvious. Read the text carefully, noting each word and making sure you understand what it is doing in the context in which you find it. As an illustration of this procedure, take a familiar passage such as the Beatitudes and begin to analyze and think about it as you may never have done before.

You may think that you already understand Matthew 5, since you probably at some point memorized the Beatitudes. In fact, the whole chapter is very familiar. But read it carefully, particularly noting what Jesus is attempting here. The clue, I believe, is in verse 20. There Jesus contrasts His kind of righteousness with that concept which was prevalent in His day and was epitomized in the teachings of the Pharisees—righteousness by works.

What are the Beatitudes all about, then? Obviously what Jesus is doing is teaching the people how to develop that righteousness which alone can bring them true happiness.

The first step in achieving the kind of happiness that Jesus makes possible in the Christian life is found in the first beatitude.

With that in mind we look carefully at every word in Matthew 5:3, trying to understand why it is there and what it is saying.

First comes the word "blessed," or happy. Who is happy? "The poor in spirit"! Isn't that strange! Certainly a person cannot be happy *because* he is poor in spirit. Notice that he is not just happy because he is poverty-stricken. Jesus was talking about the poor *in spirit*—the spiritually poor. Not because they *are* in that condition, but because they recognize it and really want to do something about it. They realize how empty they are without Him and are determined to find Him.

What is the result? "Their's *is* the kingdom of heaven." The word "is" suggests that all who realize their need and turn to Christ are presently and continually finding this need supplied.

Theirs is the positive assurance that they belong to Christ's kingdom now. He doesn't just promise some future utopia. Heaven begins here and now when we partake with Christ of His kingdom.

As you continue to look carefully at the meaning and significance of each word in this text, you will probably notice that it specifically states that the *kingdom* is theirs. They are not addressed just as subjects but as *partakers*—joint heirs with Christ. Actually this kingship is *our* kingship, as we share with Him all the privileges of being sons and daughters of God.

The next step in this kind of careful, thoughtful attention to the text is to turn to what others can help us discover. We have found what we can for ourselves. Now by turning to the right sources we can still learn more.

First, we turn to the inspired commentary—the spirit of prophecy. For this text we naturally refer to *Thoughts From the Mount of Blessing*. Pages 6 through 9 give us interesting background and confirm our discovery that the "poor in spirit" Christ is talking about are those who have learned that they cannot possibly save themselves or perform any righteous action. They are completely dependent on what Christ can do for them.

We also learn (page 13) that "throughout the beatitudes is an advancing line of Christian experience." This gives us the key to the beatitudes. They are the sequential steps we take. Therefore, the first beatitude is the first essential step—recognition of our need.

Don't stop now! Really, you are just getting started. There is a lot more help available. You could find other spirit of prophecy references that might enable you to learn more about what the "kingdom of heaven" is all about and substantiate the fact that we can experience it now. (See *The Desire of Ages,* p. 388).

Probably the next source most Adventists would turn to is the *S.D.A. Bible Commentary.* Passages in volume 5, pages 324, 325 and 1083, 1084, are particularly helpful. There we read that "the kingdom Christ came to establish was one that begins within men's hearts, permeates their lives, and overflows into other men's hearts and lives with the dynamic and compelling power of love."—Page 325.

A few may have access to the many tools available to help understand the meaning of the original Greek text. How rich this text becomes when we realize that the word used for "poor" is not just the ordinary word, but the one used to designate the desperate and destitute. Thus we learn that Jesus is literally telling us how *beggars* can become *kings.* The position of the pronoun "theirs" in the Greek text gives it particular emphasis. *Only those* who have the kind of experience outlined in this passage—who realize their desperate need and turn to Christ to supply it—will receive the blessing.

The Greek present tense of the verb "is" marks present, continuing reality. It emphasizes the thought that the kingdom is ours now and that it is ours continually, as long as we are in Christ.

Many other helps are available. But these are sufficient to make the point. What a depth of meaning we can find in even the most familiar texts if we will just take time to consider each word prayerfully and carefully and learn to recognize the significance of what we are looking at.

ANSWERS TO WORDS THAT HAVE CHANGED MEANING (page 49):

1. Affect (verb): to desire earnestly, seek after. Galatians 4:17.

2. Check (noun): reproof, rebuke. Job 20:3.

3. Fat (noun): a vat, vessel. Joel 2:24; 3:13.

4. Fray (verb): to frighten. Deuteronomy 28:26; Jeremiah 7:33; Zechariah 1:21.

5. Let (verb): to hinder, prevent. Exodus 5:4; Isaiah 43:13; Romans 1:13.

6. Ouches (noun plural): sockets in which precious stones are set. Exodus 28:11.

7. Prevent (verb): to do or come before, to anticipate. Psalm 18:5; 1 Thessalonians 4:15.

8. Sith (conjunction): since. Ezekiel 35:6.

6
Seeing With
a Ball Point

Do you remember what Professor Agassiz was quoted as having said in chapter 2 about using a pencil? He quipped, "A pencil is one of the best eyes." If he were with us nowadays, he'd probably rephrase that to read, "A ballpoint is one of the best eyes!" As we begin to take our Bible study more seriously, we need to form the habit of writing down what we are discovering for ourselves.

Sometimes, when giving talks on this kind of Bible study before church groups, I hold up a piece of blank paper and challenge, "What's the very best and most valuable use for this paper?"

There are innumerable uses, of course. You could wad it up and use it as a makeshift ball for an impromptu baseball game, as sometimes used to happen in my high school homeroom. Or, using a little more ingenuity, you could fold it into a paper airplane to amuse yourself with. Or if you've had some training in the Japanese art of origami, you might be able to fold the paper in such a way that you made a beautiful swan.

It could also be used to wrap something valuable in or to write directions or make a shopping list on. But what are some of the more valuable potential uses for a blank sheet of paper?

A millionaire could write a check on it. Or it could be used to write a famous and valuable autograph on. Or it might be used for a sketch by a famous artist. But an even more valuable purpose is that it could be used to save an individual or a group of individuals. Wouldn't that be by far the most valuable use? A letter might be written on it that could change someone's life. Or it could be used to write out a sermon that would over the years reach many hearts for Christ. Or a portion of the gospel might be printed on it.

Or it might be used to lead to a better understanding of God's Word. It's this last use that we're particularly thinking of here.

What a thrill it is to be able to sit down with an open Bible, a pen or pencil, a piece of paper, and the presence of the Holy Spirit and produce a record of your own personal discovery of some of the deep truths waiting to be brought to light from the Word of God. It takes application and time and effort, but nothing worthwhile is ever gained without such diligence.

"Sharp, clear perceptions of truth will never be the reward of indolence. Investigation of every point that has been received as truth will richly repay the searcher; he will find precious gems. And in closely investigating every jot and tittle which we think is established truth, in comparing scripture with scripture, we may discover errors in our interpretation of Scripture. Christ would have the searcher of his word sink the shaft deeper into the mines of truth. If the search is properly conducted, jewels of inestimable value will be found."—Ellen White, *Review and Herald*, July 12, 1898.

Sometimes just the act of organizing and setting down in a simple and descriptive manner the thoughts and ideas that come while studying will enable you to see clearly that which you might not otherwise have recognized. Also writing down or drawing or outlining what you are studying enables you later to recall more accurately that which you have discovered.

Nearly all currently available guides to in-depth Bible study include various kinds of charts, diagrams, and other such methods of writing down and analyzing the passage or passages being studied. Summarizing the reasons found in these varoius manuals, I have come up with the following list of what these techniques do. I find that they do these things:

1. Facilitate observation.
2. Crystallize thinking.
3. Help one see the total picture.
4. Enable better remembering.
5. Help avoid the superficial reasoning.
6. Become a permanent record of your thinking.
7. Create useful and effective teaching tools and outlines.

Several different kinds of charts are being introduced in this book, and we hope that you will try them. Make sure you fully understand a chart and that using it results in a better understanding of God's Word.

One of the most beneficial contributions of using such charts is that it teaches us to become careful observers of the text we're looking at. To open the Bible to the twenty-third psalm and find and quickly read through the words that have become so familiar to us may reassure us in time of stress and comfort us due to associations built up over a period of time.

But consider the following words: "The Lord is my shepherd; I shall not want. He maketh me to lie down in green pastures: he leadeth me beside the still waters." What do these words *really* mean? Why are these particular ones chosen? How do they relate to each other in this particular sequence?

Why are they important to you? What depth of beauty and thought lies beneath the familiar surface? And just how should you go about studying such a passage in depth? Obviously one important step is careful observation. To teach yourself to observe, divide a sheet of paper in three columns and give titles to the colums as follows:

Scripture Passage	Observations	Questions for Understanding

Under *Scripture Passage* write down the designation of the verse being studied; and then break this verse into units of phrases or clauses, each containing a unified idea. Leave approximately three lines of space between each so as to provide room for parallel observations and questions in the next two columns.

Using the phrases indicated above from the twenty-third psalm, you might place them in the first column, as follows:

Scripture Passage	
Psalm 23:1, 2	
The Lord is my Shepherd	
I shall not want	
He maketh me to lie down in green pastures	
He leadeth me beside the still waters	

Even this first simple step helps you to separate graphically the ideas involved in the passage. Now go back and think carefully about the significance of each clause and about the words involved. As you do so, record your observations and questions in the appropriate parallel columns.

Under *Observations* write down all meaningful ideas that come into your mind as you carefully meditate on the thought unit being studied. Particularly note any new and interesting concept contained in it.

Under *Questions for Understanding* write down all significant questions that come to your mind as you study each thought unit. If the answer is not immediately obvious, do not try to answer at this point, but leave space to fill in the answers that may become clear after you have completed the rest of the chart. Do not search out answers in source or reference materials at this point. Do your honest best to think through the answers for yourself. Even then, don't put down something that someone else has said just because he said it. Include it in your notes only if it seems logical and clear to *you*. These notes are to reflect *your* understanding—not someone else's.

One practical suggestion: If the material being studied is so familiar to you that you just can't seem to think of anything fresh, try reading it in another and less familiar version of the Bible. Above all, don't quit at this point, especially if it seems a little difficult. Most of us have to *learn* to concentrate and observe. *Pray* that the Holy Spirit will help you. *Claim* Christ's promise: "When the Spirit of truth comes, he will guide you into all the truth." John 16:13, R.S.V.

Following are some of the questions you might ask yourself and try to answer:

1. What does this clause or word really mean?

2. Why is it expressed this way? Is there a reason for this express terminology?

3. What is the author's purpose in this passage?

4. How does this relate to what has gone before or follows?

5. Is this word a key word? Is it especially important to this passage?

6. What is the literary structure involved? Why this structure?

7. Is it literal or symbolic?

8. What are the implications? Is there a deeper meaning than that which appears on the surface?

9. Is there progression here? Is it part of a list?

10. Who is speaking, and what is he really saying?

Of course there are scores of such questions you might ask. Don't be mechanical. Let the passage itself suggest the questions to you. But in case you just can't get started, try asking some of the above. Make sure, however, that the questions are relevant and pertinent to your study. It's easy to get sidetracked into spending a lot of time on items merely incidental to the main ideas and purpose of the passage.

7
The Search

Many years ago a man called Doc Noss found several million dollars' worth of gold bricks—at least, that's what he claimed. Doc, part Cheyenne Indian, was an agile fellow. He told any who would listen that during an outing he found the gold at the bottom of a deep cavern in the Umbrillo Basin area of New Mexico. Along with the gold, Doc said, he saw 27 human skeletons tied to posts.

But times have changed. The Umbrillo Basin section of New Mexico is now part of the United States Army's White Sands Missile Range. Rumors of the gold kept cropping up, but the Army considered the story a hoax and refused explorers entry into the area. Finally, however, a Florida-based group known as Expedition Unlimited was able to obtain approval for a search. They were not only determined to search for that gold but had $75,000 to invest in the project. Norman Scott, the leader of the group, persuaded the Army to suspend all activity on the range for ten days, giving them time to make a thorough and well-organized search of the area.

The lure of gold attracts certain kinds of individuals. Joe Newman, a carpet salesman from El Paso, Texas, put forward a claim that any gold found there belonged by right to the Apache Indians and worked out an arrangement with the tribe whereby he would receive a cut for representing their interests.

Jesse James III, grandson of the notorious outlaw, asserted that his grandfather, Jesse James I, was not killed but went underground and buried his loot in the Umbrillo Basin area.

Tony Tully, an elderly member of the expedition team, insisted that he had actually helped Doc Noss bury 110 bars of gold.

Urged on by Doc's widow, the team searched for the allotted ten days, plus an additional three that the longsuffering Army allowed. Using metal detectors, ground radar, and all the modern instruments available, they did discover many unknown tunnels and caverns. But no gold.

At the end of thirteen days the disappointed members of the team went their separate ways. Some are still convinced, however, that millions, perhaps billions, of dollars worth of gold are still there—somewhere.

As this incident illustrates, those who search for treasure hidden in the earth are often disappointed. But those who continue to put forth the necessary time and effort seeking for the treasure hidden in the Word of God will *always* find it. We are plainly told that "in God's word is found wisdom unquestionable, inexhaustible—wisdom that originated, not in the finite, but in the infinite mind."—Ellen White, *Testimonies,* vol. 6, p. 132. However, this wisdom is often buried beneath the rubbish of human wisdom and tradition; so we must perseveringly search for it. "To many the treasures of the word remain hidden, because they have not been searched for with earnest perseverance until the golden precepts were understood. The word must be searched in order to purify and prepare those who receive it to become members of the royal family, children of the heavenly King."—*Ibid.*

The promised results certainly make the time and effort expended vastly worthwhile. To some the techniques of inductive Bible study seem rather complicated, but they really aren't. After all, they are really only what we do all the time when we study the Bible. However, an attempt is made to systematize them so that we can get the most for the amount of time we spend.

Making a list may seem too simple to be of value. But it really pays. I find this out every time I go to the store without a list, for I always end up paying more than if I have one. It is interesting to note when the Bible author himself uses lists, such as Paul's listing of the fruit of the spirit in Galatians 5:22, 23 and of the heroes of faith in Hebrews 11. There's Peter's ladder of Christian experience in 2 Peter 1:5-8. Incidentally, note that it begins with faith and ends with love, just as does 1 Corinthians 13:13. Jesus listed the seven steps to becoming children of God in Matthew 5:3-9, and perhaps the most famous list of all is the Ten Commandments.

But even more interesting is finding Bible lists for yourself that are not always so obvious. Some of the kinds of things you can list are as follows:

1. Significant terms.
2. Figures of speech.
3. Lists of negative aspects and positive aspects.
4. Traits of a Bible character revealed.
5. All Bible references to a particular event or subject.
6. Attitudes revealed (each with an analysis of how it is dealt with).
7. Questions asked, by whom asked, and the answer.
8. The real messages of the passage. (List several possibilities; then select those you consider most applicable.)

There is a wide variety of possibilities in such lists. Those indicated above are merely illustrative of the great potential of this technique. Because we learn by doing, why not try making a list and finding out what we can learn from using this approach. For instance, what can we discover about Sabbath observance from listing Christ's recorded Sabbath miracles? What can we infer from the fact that only seven are listed? They are found in the following passages:

1. John 5:1-16. Pool of Bethesda, associated with the Passover of A.D. 29.

2. Mark 1:21-28. Demoniac in the synagogue, associated with the beginning of His Galilean ministry, A.D. 29.

3. Mark 1:29-31. Peter's mother-in-law, associated with the beginning of His Galilean ministry, A.D. 29.

4. Mark 3:1-6. Man with withered hand, associated with His first Galilean missionary tour, A.D. 29.

5. John 9:1-41. Man born blind, associated with the Feast of Tabernacles, A.D. 30.

6. Luke 13:10-17. Crippled woman, associated with His Peraean ministry, A.D. 31.

7. Luke 14:1-6. Healing man with dropsy, associated with His Peraean ministry, A.D. 31.

Note that the first four take place in those few months that surround the crisis at the time Jesus was rejected in Judea and the beginning of His Galilean ministry. The last three miracles take place during those months which immediately precede His crucifixion. The two recorded in Mark 1 took place on the same Sabbath, while Mark 1:32 makes it clear that Jesus waited until after sunset to heal a large crowd of people who were diseased and devil-possessed. (It is quite interesting to raise the question as to whether or not this indicates that we should exercise caution even in the work of healing on the Sabbath.) But the point here is that the simple technique of "making a list and checking it twice" can be a valuable tool in seeking and finding the gold buried in the Scripture.

Many approach Bible study in a hit-and-miss fashion. But how much more rewarding it is to follow a systematic approach. Some of the techniques I'm suggesting are, of course, not new to you; but they are an attempt to systematize an approach that will lead you to "find new glories in the word of God."—Ellen White, *Testimonies,* vol. 5, p. 266.

Comparison and contrast are often used to express our concepts so that they can be more clearly understood. In giving a description it is only natural to compare an item with something similar or even something almost the opposite. One way to increase both our understanding of Bible truth and our powers of observation is to watch for such comparisons in the Scripture. Comparing scripture with scripture is one of the most familiar Bible-study techniques. The value of such a method is outlined in Ellen White's *Fundamentals of Christian Education* (p. 187): "The Bible is its own expositor. One passage will prove to be a key that will unlock other passages, and in this way light will be shed upon the hidden meaning of the word. By comparing different texts treating on the same subject, viewing their bearing on every side, the true meaning of the Scriptures will be made evident."

One way to use this technique systematically is through the development of simple comparison charts. Such a chart can be made by dividing a page down the middle and listing on each side the items being compared or contrasted. Many varia-

Item	Nicodemus	Woman at Well
A. Type of person contacted:		
1. Age (approximate)		
2. Sex		
3. Race		
4. Position		
5. Character		
B. Approach:		
1. Initial		
2. Method of sustaining interest		
3. Creating desire		
4. Decision		
C. Result		

tions of this type of chart can be used. Use the chart on the preceding page, which compares Christ's interview with Nicodemus, recorded in John 3, with His conversation with the woman at the well, recorded in John 4. When you complete this chart, you should understand better than you have before why these chapters are side by side in the Gospel of John.

The Emphasis on Emphasis

One very interesting approach to studying the Bible passage is that of discovering what the author is emphasizing. Obviously it is extremely important in fully understanding his intent. The author may emphasize quantitatively by devoting more space to certain ideas, events, places, or persons than to others. He may also emphasize by repetition, by grammatical structure, or by other techniques.

We learn a lot about the author and about his intent by merely noting key words or phrases that are repeated over and over again. Note, for instance, how often the words "life," "belief," "witness," "light," "water," and "bread" appear in the Gospel of John. I have underlined my copy of the Revised Standard Version in accordance with the suggestion and found that the word "life" appears forty-seven times in the Gospel. Note also how many times Paul uses the phrase "in Christ" or similar phrases in Ephesians.

Joseph M. Gettys, on page 17 of his booklet *How to Enjoy Studying the Bible,* indicates that anyone desiring to use the inductive method of study must always note the following:

1. The key persons in each paragraph.
2. The key places in each paragraph.
3. The key events or happenings in each paragraph.
4. The key ideas in each paragraph.

An easy way to note these keys is to use a code of some sort for marking these key words or concepts in the margin as you read or by underlining the text. One of the clearest ways to do this is to use a different colored pencil to underline each of the four items listed above, as you discover them in the text.

Although it cannot always be substantiated that space is a key to emphasis, it is generally true that a Bible author devotes more space to those ideas, events, places, or persons with which he is primarily concerned. A simple way of determining such emphasis is to lay out a schematic diagram. For instance, one way of diagraming the emphasis on certain phases of Christ's ministry, as recorded in

Areas of Christ's Ministry	John's Record (by Chapters)
Early Years	(2:12-25)
Judean Area	1 3 5 7 8 9 10 11 12 13 14 15 16 17 18 19 20
Galilean Area	6 21
Gentile Areas	(2:1-11) (4:43-54) (4:1-42)

73

the Gospel of John, is that presented on the previous page. Note that emphasis is revealed by that which is omitted as well as by that which is included.

Another means of quantitative diagraming in the Gospel of John would be to indicate the proportion of space given to the ministry of Jesus as compared to that given to the events immediately surrounding His passion, as follows:

1	2	3	4	5	6	7	8	9	10	11	12	13	14	15	16	17	18	19	20	21
Intro-duction			Ministry									Passion							Conclu-sion	

Exegesis by Ruler

Dr. F. E. J. Harder even shows how to use a ruler as an exegetical tool. For Genesis 1:1 to 2:3 he states the following:

"With a ruler measure the column inches used to describe each day of creation week. Which day has the most space devoted to it? What fraction of the creation story is used in describing what happened on that day? What does this indicate regarding the author's purpose? In figuring this do not include the first two introductory verses of Genesis 1. Measure each day's space to the nearest one-eighth of an inch. Divide the number of inches used for the longest description of a day's work into the total to get the fraction asked for."—*Bible for Today*, p. 7.

It's an interesting exercise. Go ahead and try it. I think you'll be surprised by what you find.

8
Making the
Short Sweet

You've heard of the "short and sweet." But how do you really go about making the short sweet? This chapter is designed to help you get the most out of analyzing a brief Bible passage through the use of a chart known as the paragraph analysis chart. It may appear at first glance to be rather complicated, but it really isn't. And it will help you to trace the grammatical and thought structure of the passage you are studying. Obviously the more graphic it becomes in portraying the structure of the passage, the more useful it will be to you.

First, leave a wide left margin on your paper. Then under separate headings of "subject," "verb," and "modifiers" write down *every* word from the Bible version you are using in one of these categories, maintaining as far as possible the original sequence of the words. In developing this structural diagram you need to note the following:

1. Place all important connectives such as *and, for, but, yet* by themselves in the middle of the chart, capitalizing these words.

2. Indicate series, if any, by numbering "1, 2, 3," etc., or with brackets.

3. After going through the entire passage in this way, inserting every word somewhere in the diagram, go back and study what you have done. Underline similar words or thoughts and note their relationship. Watch for contrasts and comparisons. Use boxes, circles, arrows, colors, or any other method which may help you note these or other interesting or notable relationships.

4. Divide the passage into its natural divisions. Draw a line across the diagram between these divisions.

When you complete the above, then it is time to draw a line down the page separating the wide left margin from the analytical diagram. In this left-hand column write down a summarizing title for each division you may have made, limiting this title to as few words as possible. If necessary for clarification or future recollection of your analysis, insert subdivisions, indenting them under your titles.

A sample of the use of this technique follows. Matthew 13:44-46 has been chosen as a Bible paragraph which clearly illustrates this method of analysis.

In the following structural diagram note the following:

1. The similarity of the structure of both parables.

2. The underlining of the verbs "hath found" and "had found" to demonstrate similarity.

Titles	Subject	Verb	Modifers
Matt. 13:44	**AGAIN**		
	The kingdom of heaven	**is like unto—**	
HIDDEN TREASURE	*TREASURE*	*HID*	*IN A FIELD*
	The which		
	WHEN		
Discovery	**A man**	*hath found*	
	he	**hideth**	
		AND	for **JOY** thereof
		1. goeth and	
Recovery		**2. selleth and**	all that he hath
		3. buyeth	that field
Matt. 13:45, 46	**AGAIN**		
	The kingdom of heaven	**is like unto—**	
PEARL OF GREAT PRICE	*A MERCHANTMAN* who	*SEEKING*	*GOODLY PEARLS*
Discovery	**WHEN**		
	he	*had found*	one pearl of great price
		1. went and	
Recovery		**2. sold and**	all that he had
		3. bought	it

3. Capitalization for emphasis.

4. Circling of "joy" to demonstrate the significance of the discovery to the one finding the treasure and his willingness gladly to dispose of everything he owned in order to possess it.

5. Boxes around "all that he hath [had]" to emphasize the extent of the men's sacrifice of their own possessions.

6. The natural breaking of the passage into two divisions introduced by the same words.

7. The series of verbs indicating the steps in recovery, in each case numbered in sequence.

8. The pattern clearly outlined in the titles.

9. How glancing down the verb column gives a quick picture of actions going on in each scene.

10. How the meaning and significance of these verses stand out graphically as you look at the whole diagram.

Irving L. Jensen points out the value of the technique when he states this:

"The analytical chart, when it is made clearly and correctly, distinguishes what is primary and what is subordinate through the use of such various means as large print, bold print, underlining, circling, and the use of color pencils. The use of such visual aids during the process of study is a fruitful discipline, for it demands that the student be continually alert in evaluating the relative importance of each minute part of his study with reference to other parts and the whole."—*Independent Bible Study,* pp. 80, 81.

This is one of the most rewarding and exciting

techniques in Bible study. Why don't you try doing such a chart for yourself? Philippians 2:5-9 is a very stimulating brief Bible passage on which to try this kind of analytical diagram.

9
Pyramids, Progress, and Principles

Bible study will never become a favorite activity if it is something we have to force ourselves to do. Only when we have experienced the thrill and excitement that come from the personal discovery of new concepts, hidden truths, and special passages that seem to leap from the page and speak to our immediate needs will we become self-motivated to *want* to keep on searching the Bible for more precious treasure.

Why do hunters get up so early in the morning and even at times risk life and limb in their effort to shoot deer or whatever game they're after? Basically, I suppose it's because they find a thrill in such activity—they enjoy hunting. But they can legally hunt only during a specified season. Isn't it wonderful that there's no limit, but instead a permanent open hunting season, on the excitement of searching for that which is new and inspiring in God's Word? Since we can study and search any time we want to, why don't we do so more often? I believe that it is mainly because we get into what seems to us a boring routine and somehow bypass so much that's there waiting for our discovery when we study the Bible.

But as we learn to watch especially for the unfamiliar, even in the most familiar passages, Bible hunting takes on new meaning. Look for the unusual story or unique text you haven't noticed or heard before. Watch for something a little different from what you've always thought. Interest yourself in a minor Bible character and find out all you can about that person.

Another exciting item to watch for is a particular pattern or interesting format that a writer is using—maybe poetry or a quotation or a play on words or a figure of speech. One of the most familiar techniques that Bible writers used to build a logical, well-integrated pattern into their presentations is progression. Progressive relationships can be expressed in a series of items built in an orderly fashion one upon the other. Perhaps one of the clearest illustrations of this is the familiar passage called Peter's ladder found in 2 Peter 1:5-7. Here is not only a list of attributes essential to Christian development, but one that follows an orderly sequence, with each one building upon or developing out of that which has gone before. The first rung of the ladder is faith. Faith leads to virtue, virtue to knowledge, and so on, to the ultimate rung in the Christian experience—charity, or love.

The Bible abounds also with instances of progression in thought patterns. James 1:13-15 illustrates this. The process of temptation and its

81

results he describes as a progressive experience. First, man is "drawn away of his own lust, and enticed." Then "when lust hath conceived, it bringeth forth sin." And, finally, the result of sin is that it "bringeth forth death."

Progression may tend toward a climax, and the climax can be narrower in its focus than the broad issue upon which it is based. If this is the case, it can be graphically illustrated by means of a simple pyramid. The broader items are listed at the base and the others in ascending sequence. For instance, the creation record in Genesis 2:4-9 begins with the heavens and the earth and finally narrows down to the trees in the garden. This progression can be illustrated in a pyramid as follows:

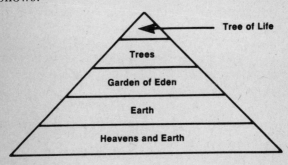

Of course some passages would lend themselves more to the use of an inverted pyramid. Look at the familiar Romans 10:14, 15, and decide what kind of pyramid you might use to portray graphically this passage.

Besides ladders and pyramids, other means of portraying progression can be used, such as the simple stairstep. Matthew 5:3-9 is a passage which we immediately recognize as a portion of the Beatitudes, but have you noticed the deep significance of these Beatitudes as the seven steps we take to becoming children of God? This might be illustrated as follows:

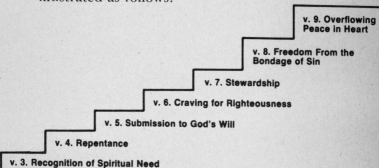

v. 9. Overflowing Peace in Heart

v. 8. Freedom From the Bondage of Sin

v. 7. Stewardship

v. 6. Craving for Righteousness

v. 5. Submission to God's Will

v. 4. Repentance

v. 3. Recognition of Spiritual Need

A more sophisticated form of progression chart is that found in the events of creation week recorded in Genesis 1:1 to 2:3. Progression is combined with comparison, as is seen in the following chart:

Progression charts are used only, of course, when the context of the passage being studied warrants such use. Many variations of the charts suggested above are possible. See what you can do to develop progression charts to illustrate Romans 5:1-5 and Matthew 11:28, 29.

As you begin putting to work some of the

83

BEGINNING—Heavens and Earth Without Form—God "Moved"		
PREPARATION	**1st Day** LIGHT INTRODUCED	**4th Day** LIGHTS IN FIRMAMENT
	2nd Day FIRMAMENT MADE WATERS UNDER FIRMAMENT	**5th Day** BIRDS IN FIRMAMENT WATER CREATURES IN SEA
	3rd Day DRY LAND APPEARED VEGETATION	**6th Day** MAN AND ANIMALS POPULATE EARTH FOOD FOR MAN AND ANIMALS
7th Day—Heavens and Earth Finished—God "Rested"		

Bible-study techniques you have been learning, you should notice a change in your attitude toward Bible study. There should be a new eagerness and air of expectancy as you open the sacred pages. Yet studying God's Word is not just a game, such as fitting a jigsaw puzzle together. It involves serious communication with the Holy Spirit and must always be approached in an attitude of prayer and true humility—remember that we're thinking God's thoughts after Him.

There are some who shy away from what I am about to suggest, but if we are careful not to abuse the privilege, we can actually be taught by the Holy Spirit as we study. Previously we suggested that we ought to let the Bible author say what he wants. Now let me suggest that we need also to let the Holy Spirit say what He wants to say.

84

The seventh chapter of Daniel presents a great outline prophecy that covers the major events of history as it relates to God's people from the time of Daniel until the establishment of Christ's everlasting dominion on earth. It was given to Daniel in the form of a dream, clothed in symbolism. Verses 15 and 16 of this chapter tell us that Daniel was troubled because he didn't understand and that he had to ask what the vision meant. In the following verses a more detailed explanation is given, but verse 28 indicates that Daniel was still very troubled.

Two years later another vision was given to Daniel. It supplemented the first vision and was designed to increase his understanding of these revelations which had been troubling him. See Daniel 8;17. Undoubtedly Daniel better understood what was to take place in the future as a result of this even more detailed explanation. But the last verse of chapter 8 relates that he fainted and was sick and astonished at the vision. Evidently he shared his perplexing visions with his friends, but they weren't able to help him understand either.

The events of chapter 9 take place about thirteen years later. Verses 2 and 3 indicate that Daniel was still troubled, mostly by the time factor involved and particularly with its relationship to the seventy-year period of captivity predicted by Jeremiah. He began to seek the answer by fasting and prayer. While he was still praying, the angel Gabriel came to his side and announced that he was there to give Daniel "skill and understanding" concerning the vision. He particularly dealt with the period of time "determined" upon Daniel's people, the Jews.

Three years later, Daniel was still so troubled about the length of time involved that chapter 10 tells us that he fasted three whole weeks over this lack of understanding. Once again he was given a vision in which he was assured of Heaven's interest in helping him to understand. Chapters 11 and 12 contain the details of this revelation, outlining events from Daniel's time to the second coming of Christ, particularly those events that the text suggests are to be sealed to the time of the end.

In Daniel 12:8 we find Daniel admitting that he could not understand these sealed events. Nor would they be understood until the last days. Daniel was told, "Go thou thy way till the end be: for thou shalt rest, and stand in thy lot at the end of the days." Verse 13. Daniel himself could not possibly fully understand the events revealed to him and recorded in the last six chapters of his book. But he was encouraged to believe that the time would come "at the end of the days" when the things he had been so troubled about would be fully understood and his writings would be unsealed and made meaningful to those who would be guided by the Holy Spirit in understanding these prophecies.

This experience of Daniel illustrates clearly the principle that even the Bible writer doesn't always fully understand the message being given through him. There are some things in the Bible that are reserved especially for readers living in the last days to understand.

Inductive Bible study first follows every possible technique to find out exactly and objectively what the author is trying to say. Next the student must realize that the Scriptures "are written for our admonition, upon whom the ends of the world are come." 1 Corinthians 10:11. Some are afraid of this step as being too subjective, and too much subjectivity can be dangerous. However it must be admitted that the Holy Spirit often intends a passage to have more than one application. Jesus Himself clearly had two applications in mind in Matthew 24—one to the time of the destruction of Jerusalem and the other to that period which immediately precedes His second coming.

Whenever a later inspired writer is led by the Holy Spirit to convey what God intended in a Bible passage, we have inspired authority for understanding it in this sense, even though the earlier author may not have thus understood it. We can go yet one step farther. The Holy Spirit is given *directly* to the church as God's special gift to guide us into all truth. John 16:13.

The Holy Spirit is not given as a shortcut to eliminate the necessity of careful and methodical study. But when we apply ourselves to thorough, methodical study as a "workman that needeth not to be ashamed," we rightly divide, or properly understand, the word of truth. 2 Timothy 2:15. Still, to approach the study of the Bible with the human mind unaided by the Holy Spirit is to open the way for a spirit not of God to control our understanding. This danger is made plain in the following statement:

"Without the guidance of the Holy Spirit we shall be continually liable to wrest the Scriptures or to misinterpret them. There is much reading of the Bible that is without profit and in many cases is a positive injury. When the word of God is opened without reverence and without prayer; when the thoughts and affections are not fixed upon God or in harmony with His will, the mind is clouded with doubt; and in the very study of the Bible, skepticism strengthens. The enemy takes control of the thoughts, and he suggests interpretations that are not correct."—Ellen White, *Testimonies,* vol. 5, pp. 704, 705.

In following the guidance of the Holy Spirit in applying biblical passages to our own time and circumstances, two factors must always be kept in mind:

First, we must be able to *distinguish* between universal principles and local applications of these principles. Certain portions of the Scripture were written to meet particular circumstances and specific instances. The principles behind the specific applications expressed in these portions are universal in their scope. But all specific applications to local circumstances and specific times and events are not necessarily applicable today.

Second, we must be able to relate a particular biblical passage to current times and circumstances. We must be able to see the relationship of truths or teachings in the passage to the Scriptures as a whole. Any one passage may emphasize a certain phase of a Bible teaching without giving all the other facets that must be understood to see the truth being discussed in its wholeness. Therefore, before drawing any definite conclusions concerning the nature of a revealed truth, it is essential to study it in the light of the entire Bible teaching on the subject. In doing so we must recognize that the Holy Spirit does not contradict Himself. Such comparative study necessitates careful thought and research, but it is worth the effort. And it is a safeguard against misinterpreting or misunderstanding a Bible teaching.

10
Putting It All Together

When I was a boy, I loved taking things apart—particularly clocks. All the wheels and gears and other pieces were fascinating to me. But putting them all back together was something else! I had parts and pieces scattered everywhere. But I could not restore too many mechanical objects to the purpose for which they were originally intended.

We don't want to tinker with Bible passages in that way, tearing them apart and analyzing them without putting them back together again. It's possible to become so involved with the single words and phrases of a Bible passage that we might completely overlook what God is basically trying to say to us.

How, then, do we go about putting it all back together again? How do we set it all in the right framework so that we see all the component parts in their beautifully integrated relationship to each other?

Summarizing individual verses, a technique we have previously described, helps us understand more readily what these verses are all about. But we also need to see them as part of their larger context. One most helpful exercise in accomplishing this is to attempt to summarize the entire scriptural section—whether it be a few verses, a whole chapter, or even an entire Bible book—in just a sentence or two, striving to capsulize the author's concept in our own words. At times we might develop a simple chart that succinctly summarizes the passage.

For instance, Matthew 24:32 through Matthew 25 contains seven parables or illustrations teaching preparedness and what it means to watch and be ready for the second coming of Christ. Attempting to summarize these in as few words as possible can be quite a challenge. After nearly an entire class period of working on this project, one of my classes came up with the following chart:

A more detailed summary chart also can be helpful, providing that it's kept to a single page. What I have come to call the "Inductive Study Chart" is useful for viewing the entire Bible section being studied and also for enabling you to visualize the whole scope of your study. This chart incorporates the horizontal summary chart concept outlined in chapter 4 and the observation chart in chapter 6 and adds a column for applications. So it becomes the culminating or final record chart that puts everything together.

Some time ago my wife and I spent a weekend with the Frederick, Maryland, church in a mountain retreat in Pennsylvania studying together

PARABLES OF PREPAREDNESS	MEANING OF "WATCH"	ATTITUDE
24:32-35—Fig Tree	Nearness	Awareness
24:36-42—As in Days of Noah	Unexpectedness	Watchfulness
24:43, 44—Thief in the Night	Unexpectedness	Readiness
24:45-51—Two Types of Servants	Responsibility	WANT Him to come
25:1-13—Ten Virgins	Spiritual Responsibility	Consecration, dedication
25:14-30—Talents	Diligence (Stewardship)	Loving anxiety to share
25:31-46—Sheep and Goats	Love	As Christ loved

how to get the most out of Bible study. When we reached the point you are at now in your study of this book, we asked the people to apply what they had been learning to a study of Psalm 1. I think you'll be quite interested in reviewing the results of our collective study as it appears in the Inductive Study Chart which follows. Note particularly the application column and how it is used.

Undoubtedly as you have practiced the methods suggested in the previous chapters, you have become involved in making applications to your own situation or to that of your family or church group. But in order to get the most out of letting the Holy Spirit say what He intends to say

PSALM 1 — THE TWO WAYS

DIVI-SION	VERSE	SENTENCE SUMMARY	QUESTIONS AND OBSERVATIONS	APPLICATION
1-3—The Way of the Righteous	1	Happiness comes from not being ungodly, sinful, or scornful.	**Degrees** *of wickedness* / *of participation* ungodly — walketh sinners — standeth scornful — sitteth **Righteousness is here described first in negatives.**	Righteousness = True happiness God is fair; He desires our happiness.
	2	Instead, one continually finds his pleasure in the revealed will of God.	Law = whole Torah. Constant pleasure in reflecting on it = delight. Preoccupied with it. In this verse righteousness is described in positives.	By beholding we become changed. Need for continuous meditation.
	3	Like a good tree he bears fruit, and the Lord blesses his life.	*Planted*—not accidentally growing—being carefully tended. River = water of life—Holy Spirit's ministry. Three blessings—good fruit in *season* doesn't wither shall prosper	Results of the godly life are as certain as good fruit is on a carefully tended tree.
4, 5—The Way of the Ungodly	4	Wicked are like the chaff, transient and worthless. They're rootless.	NOT SO = Contrast Tree held prisoner by its roots but in reality grows and bears fruit. Chaff is *free* but in reality a slave to environment and sin. TREE = LONG LIFE/CHAFF = TRANSIENT	We must be rooted and grounded in Jesus if we are to bear fruit and lead worthwhile lives.
	5	The ungodly cannot stand in the judgment.	Must be a separation—each finds his own level. Sinners = those who miss the mark. The wicked can't take the heat!	It is because of their lack of stability and interest that the ungodly cannot eternally associate with God and His people.
6—Summary: Eternal Results	6a	Way of righteous: God knows	God KNOWS the natural results of our choices far better than we can know. They are revealed in the verses above. His people prosper eternally.	In His love He seeks to let us know.
	6b	Way of ungodly: shall perish	Separation from all that is worthwhile, eternally. The second death.	God tells us clearly so that we can make the right and intelligent choice.

through the passage you are studying, it will probably be helpful to have a guide that can suggest certain questions you might ask as you make applications. After working with these for a while, it will become second nature to ask such questions on your own. But at first you should consult the list if for no other reason than to form the habit of checking yourself to make sure you are doing a thorough enough job in this respect. The following list is suggested by Oletta Wald on pages 44 and 45 of *The Joy of Discovery:*

1. **Faith.** What does the Bible passage teach me about personal faith? What do I learn about God, Jesus Christ, the Holy Spirit, and my relationship to Them? What specific truths should I believe? Why should I believe them?

2. **Attitudes.** What do I learn about good or bad attitudes? What are the results of each kind? What should be my attitudes? How can I change negative ones? What do I learn about emotions? Is there help suggested for release from destructive emotions such as fear, worry, anxiety, hate, resentment, jealousy?

3. **Actions.** What should be my actions? Are there errors to avoid? Are there any actions which I need to change?

4. **Sins.** What sins are pointed out in my life? Are there some which I need to confess to God? To my fellowmen? Are there some which I need to forsake?

5. **Examples.** What examples are there to follow? Not to follow? Why?

94

6. **Challenges.** What are some admonitions which I should make my own? How can I follow these admonitions in a concrete way in my relationships in my home? in school? at work? with others? with friends?

7. **Promises.** What promises can I claim for my own? Are there any conditions which I must fulfill in order to claim these promises? Are there any specific prayer promises to claim?

Remember, as you follow the above suggestions, that only as the Holy Spirit guides you will your applications be truly pertinent to your life situation. Ask yourself, "What would happen if I really practiced what I am reading here? What would I do that is different from what I am doing now?" Try to be as objective as possible. It is not easy to let the Holy Spirit guide us, "for the word of God is quick, and powerful, and sharper than any twoedged sword, piercing even to the dividing asunder of soul and spirit, and of the joints and marrow, and is a discerner of the thoughts and intents of the heart." Hebrews 4:12.

11
Words to Grow By

The old adage "we are what we eat" can apply not only to the physical dimension of life but to the spiritual as well. If our spiritual diet is impoverished and we try to feed our souls on the husks of the commonplace and uninspired, our minds and souls will become dwarfed and cheapened.

Do you know someone who in the last few years has demonstrated striking Christian growth? If you check the reason for it, I'm sure that you'll discover that deep, daily, and prayerful Bible study underlies all such spectacular Christian development. Peter counsels, "As newborn babes, desire the sincere milk of the word, that ye may grow thereby." 1 Peter 2:2. And Jesus informed the devil, "Man shall not live by bread alone, but by every word that proceedeth out of the mouth of God." Matthew 4:4.

What this book has been all about is demonstrating how you can develop a real appetite for Bible study in a practical way. Two counsels from the Lord especially indicate the need for doing so.

The first tells us the following: "If the people of God would appreciate His word, we should have a heaven in the church here below. Christians would be eager, hungry, to search the word. They would be anxious for time to compare scripture with scripture and to meditate upon the word. They would be more eager for the light of the word than for the morning paper, magazines or novels. Their greatest desire would be to eat the flesh and drink the blood of the Son of God. And as a result their lives would be conformed to the principles and promises of the word. Its instruction would be to them as the leaves of the tree of life. It would be in them a well of water, springing up into everlasting life. Refreshing showers of grace would refresh and revive the soul, causing them to forget all toil and weariness. They would be strengthened and encouraged by the words of inspiration."—Ellen White, *Testimonies,* vol. 8, p. 193.

Isn't that an exciting promise? Through a return to careful Bible study we can have "a heaven in the church here below" and actually partake of the "leaves of the tree of life" now.

The second major reason for us as church members to become especially familiar with the Bible at this time is so that we may clearly distinguish the false from the true in this age when we're being besieged on every side by insidious teachings.

For decades the Western world has been so wrapped in the stifling cocoon of technology that

97

religion has been pretty well excluded from everyday life and thought. Because of the tremendous promise of scientific advance, a large number of people decided they didn't need God or the hope of a future heaven. Why, heaven was to be established on earth right now!

Then technology seemed to turn on us. Nuclear weapons, environmental pollution, and cancer-producing agents in many things technology has provided pulled out all our props and left us with uncertainty and fear.

Since the old values had been thrown away, modern man was left with no place to turn; and the devil—actually a large number of devils—has filled the vacuum. This is evident in the current popularity of the occult, astrology, oriental mysticism, TM, and the rise of the cults. We are now surrounded by a growing bombardment of daily satanic lies.

Therefore, it is truer than it ever has been that "we need to search the Scriptures daily, that we may know the way of the Lord, and that we be not deceived by religous fallacies. The world is full of false theories and seductive spiritualistic ideas, which tend to destroy clear spiritual perception, and to lead away from truth and holiness. Especially at this time do we need to heed the warning, 'Let no man deceive you with vain words' (Eph. 5:6)."—Ellen White, *Selected Messages,* bk. 1, p. 170.

The tragedy today is that even among those Christians who without question receive the Bible "as it is in truth, the word of God" (1 Thessalonians 2:13) so many neglect to follow the example of the Thessalonians and give it a chance to work "effectually" in them.

It isn't so much that we don't feel the need, but too often we just don't quite know how to go about getting the most out of the time we do spend with the Bible. We know it's "good for us"; so we make a valiant attempt to read as much as we can. But this kind of forced study doesn't really do much good. It is only as we learn to discover for ourselves what God is trying to communicate to us and become so thrilled about it that we take time to dig below the picked-over surface of the Bible treasure chest that we can find words to grow by every day as we turn to the Bible.

One final caution. The wide variety of techniques described in the foregoing pages should not leave you with the impression that you *must* use all of them and use them frequently in order to "get the most out of Bible study." What we hope you'll do is try each of them and discover for yourself those that you can most readily use and that are of particular benefit to your individual study program. You'll undoubtedly adapt many of them to meet your particular needs, and this is exactly what we want you to do. Never, never use them just because you think you're supposed to!

I've described those techniques that have helped me gain new insights and have given me great pleasure as I have used them in my personal study. As I've shared them with others over the past several years, they tell me that many of them work nicely for them too. Of course, each is designed for a particular use; and you'll have to learn from experience how to use the right tool for the right job—how to apply the right technique to the particular kind of Scripture passage you're dealing with.

But most of all we trust that as you begin to apply the techniques of Bible study we've shared, the Bible will become more alive for you than it ever has been. But even that is not enough. No matter how much you come to enjoy Bible study, unless it brings about a change in your thinking and in your pattern of living, it has not accomplished what God intends it to. However, if you faithfully apply yourself to careful study, you can certainly expect the fulfillment of the promise that "he who opens the Scriptures, and feeds upon the heavenly manna, becomes a partaker of the divine nature."—Ellen White, *Review and Herald,* June 28, 1892.

Only need-motivated and God-directed Bible study brings us God's words—words to live and grow by.

Appendix

OUR FABRIC OF FAITH: A CASE STUDY OF HABAKKUK

Introduction

The only good way I know of finding answers is to ask questions. Yet most of us feel hesitant about questioning God.

Of course, there are at least two kinds of questioning. There's the skeptical, doubting kind that reinforces our inclination not to believe. On the other hand, the right kind of questioning is necessary if faith is to grow. Apparently God is pleased to answer the last-mentioned kind of questions. He illustrates this willingness in the book of Habakkuk, a much-neglected but all-important Bible book found among the so-called minor prophets. Through it all we sense God's eagerness to help us develop a strong faith.

In a period of deep apostasy Habakkuk became

exceedingly concerned about two aspects of God's dealings with his nation that he could not understand. The entire book that is called by this prophet's name is devoted to these two questions and God's answers and concludes with Habakkuk's joyous expression of the great faith he developed as a consequence of his fascinating dialogue with God.

What a privilege it is for us to be able to follow this dialogue! The questions Habakkuk raised are as pertinent, if not more so, today as they were when he first dared to raise them.

The pages which follow are intended to give you practical experience in using the Bible-study method developed in the main body of this book. If you come across an unfamiliar chart or technique, review the appropriate part of the book for an explanation of how to use it.

The **Study Guide to Habakkuk** is provided in the hope that as you get involved with an in-depth study of a short Bible book, you will be stimulated to apply these same techniques as you continue to study the rest of the Bible.

After the study guide we have included an answer sheet; but we strongly recommend that you not even look at those pages until you have completed your own study. Then, as you compare your answers with ours, you will see that you have discovered for yourself the basic meaning of a passage, even though it will naturally differ somewhat from what we have discovered as we looked at the same passage.

Study Guide to Habakkuk

From personal observation of the portion of scripture you are studying and from Bible dictionaries or Bible commentaries, complete this study-guide outline by answering the questions, completing the charts, and giving word or short-sentence answers.

I. Background (see chapter 4 for more detailed information)
   A. Authorship
      1. Who was the author?
      2. At what time in his life was he writing?
      3. Where was he when he wrote the material?
      4. What characteristics of the author are revealed here?
      5. What was he experiencing at the time he wrote this section?
      6. What is the underlying tone of the passage?
   B. Purpose
      1. What do historical records indicate as background for this section?
      2. What contribution do archaeological findings make?
      3. What is the author's primary purpose in writing this book?

4. What are the major truths or concerns and convictions which he is presenting in order to bring out his purpose?

5. How has he arranged his material to emphasize his purpose?

6. What are the key words he uses?

7. Who are the intended readers, and how does this affect his purpose?

8. How does this emphasis compare with other works of this period (by the same author or other authors)?

C. Complete the following horizontal summary chart.

1:2-2:1 =	2:2-20 =	3:1-19 =
Habakkuk—1:2-5	verses 2-5	1-15
	6-8	
God—1:6-11	9-11	
	12-14	16
	15-17	
Habakkuk—1:12-2:1	18, 19	17-19
	20	

II. Analysis

A. Make a paragraph-analysis chart for Habakkuk 2:2-5 (see chapter 8 for information on how to develop this chart).

	verses 2, 3 And the *Lord* answered me . . .
	verse 4 Behold . . .
	verse 5 Moreover . . .

B. List the words and phrases which describe the Chaldeans in 1:5-11.

C. Compare 1:4 with 2:4.

QUESTIONS	1:4	2:4
Who is speaking?		
What is the position of the unjust?		
What is the position of the righteous?		

D. Can you see any relationship between 2:20 and each of the five woes (2:6-19)?
1. 1st—
2. 2nd—
3. 3rd—
4. 4th—
5. 5th—

E. Try to determine from the context what is meant by the following figures of speech.

1. 2:9—"To set his next on high."

2. 2:11—"The stone will cry out from the wall, and the beam from the woodwork respond."

3. 2:13—"Peoples labor only for fire."

4. 2:16—"The cup in the Lord's right hand will come around to you."

F. Note the progression of the prophet's attitude toward God in the following verses.

1. 1:2, 3—

2. 1:12-17—

3. 2:1—

4. 3:2—

5. 3:16—

6. 3:17-19—

G. What do the following terms mean in chapter 3?

1. verse 1. Shigionoth.

2. verse 3. Teman.

3. verse 4. Rays flashed from His hand.

4. verse 7. Cushan.

5. verse 9. Selah.

6. verse 19. The last six words (R.S.V.)—in relationship to the rest of the chapter.

H. In the first column of the following chart list all phrases in chapter 3 which apply to the glory and saving activities of God. In the second column list all phrases applying to the wrath and judgment activities of God.

Glory and Salvation	Violence and Judgment

I. Complete the following chart using all pertinent portions of chapter 3.

Areas Involved	Objects of Glory and Salvation	Objects of Violence and Judgment
Heaven		
Earth		
People		

III. Summary

    A. Summarize in one complete sentence the basic philosophy of the book of Habakkuk.

    B. Apply the basic principles involved in the following to the Christian today.

       1. Habakkuk's questions.

       2. God's answers.

       3. Habakkuk's psalm.

Suggested Answers for Study Guide

I. Background

A. Authorship

1. Who was the author? *Not much revealed in book. Prophet-philosopher. Perhaps a priest, but at least a temple singer (chapter 3).*

2. At what time in his life was he writing? *Period of deep apostasy–perhaps earliest years of Josiah's reign (PK 386).*

3. Where was he when he wrote the material? *Judah–most probably in Jerusalem area.*

4. What characteristics of the author are revealed here? *Philosophical turn of mind. Basic confidence in God which gives him courage to question God. Lover of peace (1:3).*

5. What was he experiencing at the time he wrote this section? *A crisis in personal faith that led to development of even stronger faith.*

6. What is the underlying tone of the passage? *It is relevant to us because it is a book of WHYS.*

B. Purpose

1. What do historical records indicate as background for this section? *Before rise of Babylonian Empire (before 625 B.C.).*

2. What contribution do archaeological findings make? *Dead Sea Scrolls contain a Habakkuk scroll dating from c. 100 B.C. (first 2 chapters).*

3. What is the author's primary purpose in writing this passage? *That the Jews might better understand God's purpose in the Babylonian captivity. Demonstrates God in control of what happens to His people.*

4. What are the major truths or concerns and convictions which he is presenting in order to bring out his purpose? *Faith in God leads to life; rebellion and wickedness lead to death.*

5. How has he arranged his material to emphasize his purpose? *(See chart on p. ??.)*

6. What are the key words he uses? *iniquity, violence, judgment, woe, salvation, trust, rejoice.*

7. Who are the intended readers, and how does this affect his purpose? *Jews—but God's intent includes us.*

8. How does this emphasis compare with the other works of this period (by the same author or other authors)? *A synopsis of the gospel, as developed to a larger extent in Isaiah. More hopeful than judgment portrayed in Nahum.*

8—H.G.M.

C. Complete the following horizontal summary chart.

HABAKKUK—GOD'S JUSTICE VINDICATED

1:2-2:1=Questionings of Faith	2:2-20=God's Answer	3:1-19=Confidence Expressed
Habakkuk—1:2-4 Question 1. Why do the wicked prosper?	**verses 2-5** The just shall live by faith, but the wicked shall fail by the inherent nature of evil.	**1-15** Introduction (vs. 1)—psalm to be musically accompanied. Description of second coming. Christ comes for the salvation of His people.
	6-8 1st WOE: (Woes illustrate the inherent destructiveness of evil.) Violence reaps violence.	
God—1:6-11 God's First Answer. The wicked in Judah will be punished by the Babylonians.	**9-11** 2d WOE: Covetousness leads to dissatisfaction with that gained thereby.	**16** Awe Humility } expressed by Habakkuk as he determines to Patience let God's will be done.
	12-14 3d WOE: Absolute power corrupts absolutely (14=parenthesis)	
	15-17 4th WOE: Three-martini business lunch condemned!	**17-19** Paean of Praise—No matter what happens, I'll rejoice in God. He is my strength and will make me tread in high places.
Habakkuk—1:12-2:1 Question 2. Why do You use a more-wicked people as Your instrument of punishment?	**18, 19** 5th WOE: Those who worship dumb idols can expect only dumb results. **20** God is still in control, and His universal laws determine men's consequences. When we understand this, our questions will be stilled.	

II. Analysis

A. Make a paragraph-analysis chart for Habakkuk 2:2-5.

	verses 2, 3
THE VISION	And the Lord answered me:
Plain	Write the vision so he may run who reads it. Make it plain upon tablets

Certain	*FOR STILL*
	The vision awaits its time,
	               hastens to the end,
	               will not lie.
	(If it seem slow, wait for it,)
	               will surely come,
	               will not delay.

	verse 4
CONTRAST IN DESTINY	Behold:
of wicked	He (whose soul is not shall fail. upright in him)
of righteous	*BUT* (most important word in book, answers all questions) the righteous (one) shall live by his faith

	verse 5
REASON **Destruction is natural result of evil.**	Moreover:
	Wine (wealth) is treacherous (deceitful).

	Arrogant man shall not abide.
	  His greed is as wide as Sheol;
	  (it) like death never has enough.

	He gathers all nations for himself, collects all peoples as his own

B. List the words and phrases which describe the Chaldeans in 1:5-11:

> They are a bitter and hasty nation.
> They seize habitations not their own.
> They are dread and terrible.
> Their sense of justice is typical of their character.
> They proudly ride their swift and fierce horses, riding forth for violence.
> They strike terror in those whom they approach.
> They take innumerable captives and scoff at other kings and rulers.
> They laugh at all fortresses and take them.
> They offend.
> They worship their power.

C. Compare 1:4 with 2:4:

Questions	1:4	2:4
Who is speaking?	Habakkuk	God
What is the position of the unjust?	Rule	Shall fail
What is the position of the righteous?	Surrounded by wicked	Shall live by faith

How do you account for the difference?

> Habakkuk judges by superficial and transitory appearance.
> God sees the end from the beginning.

D. Can you see any relationship between 2:20 and each of the five woes?

1. *1st–The God who controls all has established a law that plunder is not enduring and those violated take their own revenge.*

2. *2nd–God in His temple hears the cry of the defrauded and has decreed that ill-gotten gain will not satisfy those who obtain it.*

3. *3rd–God's heart sympathizes with the victims of cruelty. Those who form empires on violence and greed build on shaky foundations.*

4. *4th–God sees that shame will come on those who take unfair advantage.*

5. *5th–Man's worship of self and God is foolish in the light of God's presence and control of things on earth.*

E. Try to determine from the context what is meant by the following figures of speech:

1. 2:9—"To set his nest on high." *Those who set their house or household on a level they consider to be safe from harm.*

2. 2:11—"The stone will cry out from the wall, and the beam from the woodwork respond." *Those who have defrauded others to build their "nests" will find their dwellings "haunted" by those they have robbed to build them.*

3. 2:13—"Peoples labor only for fire." *Fire-destruction, both literally and eschatologically. This is better understood by parallelism—"weary themselves for very vanity."*

4. 2:16—"The cup in the Lord's right hand will come around to you." *The cup is God's wrath.*

F. Note the progression of the prophet's attitude toward God in the following verses:

1. 1:2, 3—*I cry; you won't listen,
   I cry; you won't save.*

2. 1:12-17—*You just can't mean what
   you're saying;
   Your eyes are too pure to favor
   evildoers.*

3. 2:1—*I'm sure the Lord will rebuke me,
   But I'm going to watch for the
   intriguing answer I know He'll
   give me.*

4. 3:2—*I have heard the hearing of you,
   and I was afraid.
   Cause Your work to come to life.*

5. 3:16—*I tremble and am weak, yet I will
   quietly wait for the fulfillment of
   God's plans.*

6. 3:17-19—*From now on, no matter what terrible thing might happen, I will trust and rejoice in the Lord.*

G. What do the following terms mean in chapter 3?·

1. Verse 1. Shigionoth. *Musical instrument of dithyramb.*

2. Verse 3. Teman. *Edom area. (See Isa. 63:1.) Enemies—those that put Christ to death.*

3. Verse 4. Rays flashed from his hand. *Tokens of Calvary are Christ's glory and highest honor.*

4. Verse 7. Cushan. *Neighbors of Edom—God's enemy.*

5. Verse 9. Selah. *Pause or flourish of trumpets when God speaks.*

6. Verse 19. Last six words (R.S.V.)—in relationship to the rest of the chapter. *A notation concerning the use of this hymn.*

H. In the first column of the following chart list all phrases in chapter 3 which apply to the glory and saving activities of God. In the second column list all phrases applying to the wrath and judgment activities of God.

Glory and Salvation	Violence and Judgment
Mercy His glory covered the heavens The earth was full of His praise His brightness like the light Rays flashed from His hand Veiled His power Went forth for the salvation of Thy people; Thy annointed	Wrath Before Him—pestilence Plagues followed close behind Measured the earth, shook the nations Mountains were scattered Hills sank low Tents of Cushan, Midian afflicted Anger against rivers Indignation against sea Thou didst ride in victory, unsheath Thy bow, put arrows to the string, cleave the earth with rivers The mountains writhed Raging waters swept on The deep gave forth its voice Sun and moon stood still Flash of Thy glittering spear Thou didst bestride the earth in fury trample the nations in anger crush the head of the wicked lay him bare from thigh to neck

I. **Complete the following chart using all pertinent portions of chapter 3.**

Areas Involved	Objects of Glory and Salvation	Objects of Violence and Judgment
Heaven	*Heavens (probably stellar)*	*Sun* *Moon*
Earth	*Earth*	*Earth* *Mountains* *Rivers* *Sea* *Deep (waters)*
People	*God's People* *His anointed*	*Nations* *Heathen* *Wicked* *Wicked warriors*

III. Summary

A. **Summarize in one complete sentence the basic philosophy of the book of Habakkuk:**

   The self-destruction of sin and selfishness is inherently at work and will bring about the ultimate destruction of those involved, but God is at work for those who turn to Him and will save them.

B. **Apply the basic principles involved in the following to the Christian today.**

   1. Habakkuk's questions. *Why does wickedness seem to prosper both inside and outside the church? Does it pay to give everything to God? Why does modern Babylon make such an impact and God's people so little?*

   2. God's answers. *WAIT AND SEE. I'm in the temple. Soon all will be made plain and right. Sin and sinners are already at work destroying themselves. The righteous will live eternally. In the end all will turn out right.*

   3. Habakkuk's psalm. *No matter what appearances may be, let's not be deceived. Trust in God. Christ our blessed hope will soon come for the salvation of His people. Then we will tread the high places with Him. (Here trumpets should sound and bells should ring!)*